Best Garden Plants for Iowa

my our garden → is on p. 448!

Chuck Porto • Laura Peters

LONE PINE

Lone Pine Publishing International

Distributed by Lone Pine Publishing
1808 B Street NW, Suite 140
Auburn, WA, USA 98001

Website: www.lonepinepublishing.com

Library and Archives Canada Cataloguing in Publication

Porto, Chuck, 1964–
    Best garden plants for Iowa / Chuck Porto, Laura Peters.

    Includes index.
    ISBN-13: 978-1-55105-520-6
    ISBN-10: 1-55105-520-1

    1. Plants, Ornamental—Iowa. 2. Gardening—Iowa.
    I. Peters, Laura, 1968– II. Title.
SB453.2.I8P48 2005   635'.09777   C2005-901641-8

Scanning & Electronic Film: Elite Lithographers Co.

Front cover photographs by Tamara Eder and Tim Matheson except where noted. Clockwise from top right: Graham Thomas shrub rose, flowering crabapple, bearded iris, lilac, daylily 'Dewey Roquemore,' sweet potato vine, daylily 'Janet Gayle' (Allison Penko), lily (Laura Peters), tickseed, lily (Erika Flatt).

Photography: All photos by Tamara Eder, Tim Matheson, Laura Peters and Allison Penko except: AAFC 64a; AASelection 25b; Bailey Nurseries 108, 114, 126a; Sandra Bit 137a; Brendan Casement 78b; David Cavagnaro 128a&b; Conard-Pyle Roses107b, 111a&b; David Austin Roses 110a; Therese D'Monte 138b; EuroAmerican 16a; Jen Fafard 134a; Derek Fell 11a, 93a&b, 106a, 112, 138a, 139; Erika Flatt 10a, 88a, 130a, 131b, 155a, 163b; Anne Gordon 85a&b, 168a; J.C. Bakker & Sons 107a; Duncan Kelbaugh 131a; Liz Klose 141b, 143a, 144a&b, 153a, 158a; Dawn Loewen 71a, 89a; Janet Loughrey 106b; Marilynn McAra 133, 134b, 135a&b, 136; Kim O'Leary 125a&b, 147b; Chuck Porto 1, 4, 8a, 10b, 118a; RBG/Chris Graham 117a; Robert Ritchie 35b, 38a, 45a&b, 51a&b, 67a, 70b, 82a, 92a, 96a, 101b, 103a, 116a&b, 121a; Leila Sidi 23b, 140b; Peter Thompstone 17a, 24a&b, 50a, 59b, 168b; Mark Turner 65b; Don Williamson 59a, 129b, 132a&b; Tim Wood 70a.

Map: Hardiness map based on USDA plant hardiness zones map (1990)

This book is not intended as a 'how-to' guide for eating garden plants. No plant or plant extract should be consumed unless you are certain of its identity and toxicity and of your potential for allergic reactions.

We acknowledge the financial support of the Government of Canada through the Book Publishing Industry Development Program (BPIDP) for our publishing activities.

PC: P1

Table of Contents

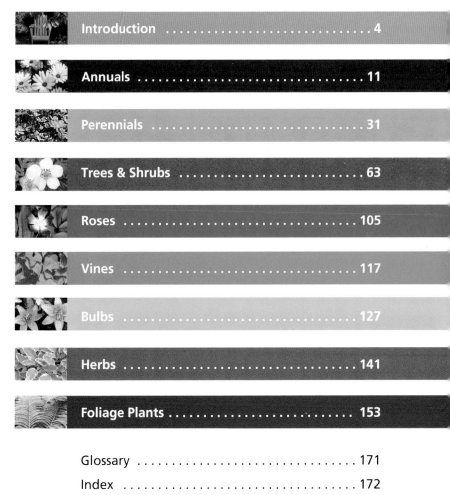

Introduction

Starting a garden can seem like a daunting task. Which plants should you choose? Where should you put them in the garden? How do you care for them? This book is intended to give beginning gardeners the information they need to start planning and planting gardens of their own. It describes a wide variety of plants and provides basic planting information, such as where and how to plant.

The weather in Iowa varies greatly from season to season, with cold winters and hot summers, with temperatures ranging from to -20° F in winter to 100° F in summer. An extreme high of 118° F was recorded in Keokuk on July 20, 1934, while the lowest recorded temperature was -47° F in Elkader on February 3, 1996. Any kind of weather is possible in the state of Iowa, but this is balanced out with an average 32" of annual precipitation and approximately 150 days of growing season.

Iowa's weather varies greatly with the seasons because it has what climatologists call a continental climate. The four distinct seasons in Iowa provide quite a bit of variety, with plenty of severe weather. In Iowa, if it isn't the heat, it's the humidity, and if you don't like the weather, wait five minutes, because it's bound to change.

Iowa's climate is characterized by warm, generally moist summers and cold winters. Temperatures vary considerably from season to season and, at times, from day to day. However, monthly averages are relatively uniform throughout the state and usually vary less than 10° F from place to place. Although total snowfall is rarely very great, the severity of the Iowa winter is often increased by high winds that produce blizzard conditions and by prolonged periods of very low temperatures. Average monthly temperatures in July range from less than 72° F in northern Iowa to more than 76° F in southern Iowa. Daytime highs in summer are usually between 85° and 90° F in most of the state. Temperatures as high as 110° F and up have been recorded, but these occur infrequently. Average January temperatures range from less than 14° F in the north to more than 24° F in the extreme southeast. In winter, nearly all places in the state may experience temperatures in the upper -20°s F range. In general, precipitation decreases from east to west. Most precipitation falls in the form of rain during spring and summer, though prolonged droughts sometimes occur in summer.

Iowa lies in the heart of the Midwest, bordered on the east by the Mississippi River and on the west by the Missouri. The landscape is generally characterized by gently rolling plains consisting mainly of open farmland, with clusters of deciduous woodland forests and crisscrossing streams to complete the picture.

Exceptions to the typical landscape are found in the northeast corner of the state, with its rock cliffs, and in the river bluffs along the eastern and western borders. Iowa's rivers feed into the Mississippi River from the eastern two-thirds of the state, and into the Missouri River mainly from the southwest portion of the state.

Geologically, Iowa is a young land. All of Iowa's surface formations were formed in the last 25,000 years—the blink of an eye in geologic time. Glaciers shaped the land during the last ice age, which ended about 10,000 years ago. The glaciers smoothed out the landscape, depositing layers of rock and debris on top of the existing sedimentary rock. The top, newest layer of earth is the rich soil of Iowa that farmers currently use to lead the nation in crop production.

Hardiness zones and frost dates are two terms often used when discussing climate. Hardiness zones consider the temperatures and conditions in winter. Plants are rated based on the zones in which they grow successfully. The last frost date in spring combined with the first frost date in fall allows us to predict the length of the growing season.

Average Annual Minimum Temperature

Zone	Temp (°F)
4a	−25 to −30
4b	−20 to −25
5a	−15 to −20

Hardiness Zones Map

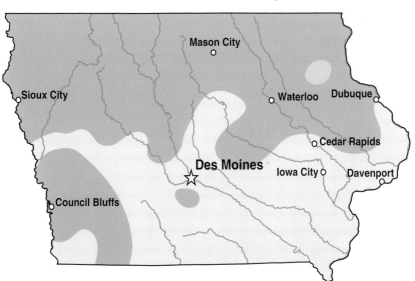

Getting Started

When planning your garden, start with a quick analysis of the garden as it is now. Plants have different requirements, so it is best to put the right plant in the right place rather than trying to change your garden to suit the plants you want.

Knowing which parts of your garden receive the most, and least, amounts of sunlight will help you choose the proper plants and decide where to plant them. Light is classified into four basic groups: full sun (direct, unobstructed light all or most of the day); partial shade (direct sun for about half the day and shade for the rest); light shade (shade all or most of the day with some sun filtering through to ground level); and full shade (no direct sunlight). Most plants prefer a certain amount of light but many can adapt to a range of light levels.

Plants use the soil to hold themselves upright, but they also rely on the many resources it holds: air, water, nutrients, organic matter and a host of microbes. The particle size of the soil influences the amount of air, water and nutrients it can hold. Sand, with the largest particles, has a lot of air space and allows water and nutrients to drain quickly. Clay, with the smallest particles, is high in nutrients but has very little air space; therefore, water is slow to penetrate clay and slow to drain from it.

Soil acidity or alkalinity (measured on the pH scale) influences the nutrients available to plants. A pH of 7 is neutral; a lower pH is more acidic. Most plants prefer a soil with a pH of 5.5–7.5. Soil-testing kits are available at most garden centers, or soil samples can be sent to testing facilities for a more thorough analysis.

Compost is one of the best and most important amendments you can add to any type of soil. Compost improves soil by adding organic matter and nutrients, introducing soil microbes, increasing water retention and improving drainage. Compost can be purchased, or you can make it in your own backyard.

Microclimates are small areas that are generally warmer or colder than the surrounding area. Buildings, fences, trees and other large structures can provide extra shelter in winter, but may trap heat in summer, thus creating a warmer microclimate. The bottoms of hills are usually colder than the tops, but may not be as windy. Take advantage of these areas when you plan your garden and choose your plants; you may even grow out-of-zone plants successfully in a warm, sheltered location.

Selecting Plants

It's important to purchase healthy plants that are free of pests and diseases. Such plants will establish quickly in your garden and won't introduce problems that can spread to other plants. You should have a good idea of what the plant is supposed to look like—its habit, and the color and

Gently remove container.

Ensure proper planting depth.

Backfill with soil.

shape of its leaves—and then inspect the plant for signs of disease or infestation.

The majority of plants are container grown. This is an efficient way for nurseries and greenhouses to grow plants, but when plants grow in a restricted space for too long, they can become pot bound, their roots densely encircling the inside of the pot. Avoid purchasing plants in this condition; they are often stressed and can take longer to establish. In some cases, they may not establish at all. It is often possible to remove pots temporarily to look at the condition of the roots. You can check for soil-borne insects and rotten roots at the same time.

Planting Basics

The following tips apply to all plants.

• Prepare the garden before planting. Dig over the soil, pull up any weeds and make any needed amendments, such as adding manure or compost, before you begin planting, if possible. This may be more difficult in established beds to which you want to add a single plant. The prepared area should be at least twice the size of the plant you want to put in, and preferably the expected size of the mature plant.

• Unwrap the roots. It is always best to remove any container before planting to give roots the chance to spread out naturally when planted. In particular, you should remove plastic containers, fiber pots, wire and burlap before planting trees. Fiber pots decompose very

slowly, if at all, and wick moisture away from the plant. Burlap may be synthetic, which won't decompose, and wire can eventually strangle the roots as they mature. The only exceptions to this rule are peat pots and pellets used to start annuals and vegetables; these decompose and can be planted with the young transplants.

• Accommodate the rootball. If you prepared your planting spot ahead of time, your planting hole will only need to be big enough to accommodate the rootball with the roots spread out slightly.

• Know the mature size. Plant based on how big plants will grow rather than how big they are when you plant them. Large plants should have enough room to mature without interfering with walls, roof overhangs, power lines and walkways.

• Plant at the same depth. Plants generally like to grow at a certain level in relation to the soil and should be planted at the same level they were at before you transplanted them.

• Settle the soil with water. Good contact between the roots and the soil is important, but if you press the soil down too firmly, as often happens when you step on the soil, you can cause compaction, which reduces the movement of water through the soil and leaves very few air spaces. Instead, pour water in as you fill the hole with soil. The water will

Settle backfilled soil with water.

Water the plant well.

Add a layer of mulch.

settle the soil evenly without allowing it to compact.

- Identify your plants. Keep track of what's what in your garden by putting a tag next to your plant when you plant it. It is very easy for beginning gardeners to forget exactly what they planted and where they planted it. Even if you always tag new transplants, each spring you will get a surprise. Either something comes back that you forgot you planted, or you just can't identify the dead brown stubs that evidently did not survive the winter.

- Water deeply and infrequently. It's better to water deeply once every week or two than to water a little bit several times a week. Watering less frequently forces roots to grow as they search for water, and it helps them survive dry spells when water bans may restrict your watering regime. Always check the rootzone before you water. More gardeners overwater than underwater. Newly planted plants should remain consistently moist and not be allowed to dry out while establishing themselves.

Annuals

Annuals are planted new each year and are only expected to last for a single growing season. Their flowers and decorative foliage provide bright splashes of color

and can fill in spaces around immature trees, shrubs and perennials.

Annuals are easy to plant and are usually sold in small packs of four or six. The roots quickly fill the space in these small packs, so the small rootball should be broken up before planting. You can often break the ball in two up the center or run your thumb up each side to break up the roots.

Many annuals are grown from seed and can be started directly in the garden.

Perennials

Perennials grow for three or more years. They usually die back to the ground each fall and send up new shoots in spring, though some are evergreen. They often have a shorter period of bloom than annuals, but require less care.

Many perennials benefit from being divided every few years. This keeps them growing and blooming vigorously, and in some cases controls their spread. Dividing involves digging the plant up, removing dead bits, breaking the plant into several pieces and replanting some or all of the pieces. Extra pieces can be given as gifts to family, friends and neighbors. Consult a perennial book for further information on the care of perennials.

Trees & Shrubs

Trees and shrubs provide the bones of the garden. They are often the slowest growing plants but usually live the longest. Characterized by leaf type, they may be deciduous or evergreen, and needled or broad-leaved.

Trees should have as little disturbed soil as possible at the bottom of the planting hole. Loose dirt settles over time and sinking even an inch can kill some trees.

Staking, sometimes recommended for newly planted trees, is only necessary for trees over 5' tall.

Pruning is more often required for shrubs than trees. It helps them maintain an attractive shape and can improve blooming. Consult a book on pruning or take a pruning course for information about pruning trees and shrubs.

Roses

Roses are beautiful shrubs with lovely, often fragrant blooms. Traditionally, most roses only bloomed once in the growing season but currently available varieties often bloom more than once during the warm summer months.

Generally, roses prefer a fertile, well-prepared planting area. A rule of thumb is to prepare an area 24" across, front to back and side to side, and 24" deep. Add plenty of compost or other fertile organic matter, and keep roses well watered during the growing season. Many roses are quite durable and will adapt to poorer conditions.

Roses, like all shrubs, have specific pruning requirements. Consult a reputable rose book for detailed information.

Vines

Vines or climbing plants are useful for screening and shade, especially in a location too small for a tree. They may be woody or herbaceous and annual or perennial.

Most vines need sturdy supports to grow up on. Trellises, arbors, porch railings, fences, walls, poles and trees are all possible supports. If a support is needed, put it in place before you plant to avoid disturbing the roots later.

Bulbs, Corms, Tubers

These plants have fleshy underground storage organs that allow them to survive extended periods of dormancy. They are often grown for the bright splashes of color their flowers provide. They may be spring, summer or fall flowering.

Hardy bulbs can be left in the ground and will flower every year, but many popular tender plants grow from bulbs, corms or tubers. These tender plants are generally lifted from the garden in fall as the foliage dies back and are stored in a cool, frost-free location for winter, to be replanted in spring.

Herbs

Herbs may be medicinal or culinary, and often are both. A few common culinary herbs are listed in this book. Even if you don't cook with herbs, the often-fragrant foliage adds different scents and aromas

unique, interesting or striking foliage in your garden can provide all the color and texture you want without the need to rely on flowers.

Ornamental grasses are becoming very popular additions to the garden. Grasses offer a variety of textures and foliage colors, and at least three seasons of interest. There is an ornamental grass for every garden situation and condition. Some grasses will thrive in any garden condition, including hot and dry to cool and wet, and in all types of soils. Ornamental grasses have very few insect or disease problems. They require very little maintenance other than cutting the perennial grasses back in fall or spring.

Ferns are ancient plants that have adapted to many different environments. The fern family is a very large group of plants with interesting foliage in a wide array of shapes and colors. Ferns do not produce flowers, but instead reproduce by spores borne in interesting structures on the undersides and margins of the foliage. Ferns are generally planted in moist, shaded gardens, but some will thrive in dry shade under dense evergreens, such as cedars and firs.

to the garden, and the plants can be quite decorative in form, leaf and flower.

Many herbs have pollen-producing flowers that attract butterflies, bees and hummingbirds to your garden. Herbs also attract predatory insects. These useful insects help to manage your pest problems by feasting on problem insects, such as aphids, mealybugs and whiteflies.

Foliage Plants

Foliage is an important consideration when choosing plants for your garden. Although many plants look spectacular in bloom, they can seem rather dull without flowers. Including a variety of plants with

We have included some grass-like foliage plants in this book. Rush has grass-like foliage and can be used with or as a substitute for ornamental grasses. We have also added a variety of plants grown for their foliage throughout the book. Many annuals, perennials, trees, shrubs, vines and herbs have wonderful foliage and will be an asset to your garden landscape.

A Final Comment

Don't be afraid to experiment. No matter how many books you read, trying things yourself is the best way to learn and to find out what will grow in your garden. Use the information provided as guidelines, and have fun!

African Daisy

Osteospermum

O. ecklonis cultivar (or Symphony Series, above), *O. ecklonis* (below)

African daisies are colorful, carefree plants that retain their good looks late into fall and can withstand temperatures as low as 25° F. New varieties have better heat and moisture tolerance.

Growing

Plant in **full sun** in **light**, evenly **moist, moderately fertile, well-drained** soil when the soil warms in spring. Do not overwater or let the plants wilt; use organic mulch to cut down on watering. Deadhead to encourage new growth and more flowers. Pinch young plants to encourage a bushier form.

Tips

African daisies work well in containers or beds. Their flowers look great mixed with plants like petunias or verbenas.

Recommended

O. ecklonis grows upright to almost prostrate, but it is often rejected in favor of its wonderful cultivars. **Passion Mix** has free-flowering, heat-tolerant plants. The **Springstar Series** boasts compact, early-flowering plants. **Starwhirls Series** flowers have unique spoon-shaped petals.

Proven Winners' *O.* **Symphony Series** has mounding plants. They tolerate heat well and flower through summer.

Also called: Cape daisy **Features:** colorful flowers; easy care; heat tolerant
Flower color: white, peach, orange, yellow, pink, lavender, purple; often with dark centers of blue purple or other colors **Height:** 12–20"
Spread: 10–20"

Ageratum
Ageratum

'Hawaii Blue' (above), *A. houstonianum* (below)

Ageratum is an amazing butterfly magnet. It offers a constant supply of nectar to many butterfly species throughout summer and fall.

Growing

Ageratum flowers best in **full sun** but tolerates partial shade. The soil should be **fertile, moist** and **well drained**. This plant doesn't like to have its soil dry out; a moisture-retaining mulch will reduce the need for water.

Tips

The smaller varieties, which are often completely covered with fluffy flowerheads, make excellent edging plants for flowerbeds and pathways. They are also attractive grouped in masses or grown in planters. The taller varieties work well in the center of a flowerbed or interplanted with other annuals. They also make interesting cut flowers.

Recommended

A. houstonianum has clusters of fuzzy, blue, white or pink flowers and forms a large, leggy mound that can grow up to 24" tall. Many cultivars are available; most, including the **Danube** and **Hawaii Series**, have a low, compact form that makes a popular choice for border plantings. Others, including '**Leilani**' and the **Horizon Series**, are much taller and make good cut flowers.

Although this plant requires deadheading to keep it flowering, the blossoms are extraordinarily long-lived.

Also called: floss flower **Features:** flowers; habit **Flower color:** white, pink, mauve, blue, purple **Height:** 6–36" **Spread:** 6–18"

Angelonia

Angelonia

A. *angustifolia* 'Blue Pacific' (above & below)

With its loose, airy spikes of orchid-like flowers, angelonia makes a welcome addition to the garden.

Growing

Angelonia prefers **full sun** but tolerates a bit of shade. The soil should be **fertile, moist** and **well drained**. Although this plant grows naturally in damp areas, such as along ditches and near ponds, it is fairly drought tolerant. Plant out after the chance of frost has passed.

Tips

Angelonia makes a good addition to an annual or mixed border, where it is most attractive when planted in groups. It is also suited to a pondside or streamside planting.

Recommended

A. *angustifolia* is a bushy, upright plant with loose spikes of flowers in varied shades of purple. Cultivars with white or bicolored flowers are available.

The individual flowers look a bit like orchid blossoms, but angelonia is actually in the same family as snapdragon.

Also called: angel wings, summer snapdragon **Features:** attractive flowers **Flower color:** purple, blue, white **Height:** 12–24" **Spread:** 12"

Bacopa

Sutera

Bacopa snuggles under and around the stems of taller plants, forming a dense carpet dotted with tiny, white to pale lavender flowers that eventually drift over pot edges to form a waterfall of stars.

Growing

Bacopa grows well in **partial shade**, with protection from the hot afternoon sun. The soil should be of **average fertility, humus rich, moist** and **well drained**. Don't allow this plant to dry out, or the leaves will quickly die. Cutting back dead growth may encourage new shoots to form.

Tips

Bacopa is a popular plant for hanging baskets, mixed containers and window boxes. It is not recommended as a bedding plant because it fizzles quickly when the weather gets hot, particularly if you forget to water. Plant it where you will see it every day so you will remember to water it.

S. cordata (above & below)

Bacopa is a perennial that is grown as an annual outdoors. It will thrive as a houseplant in a bright room.

Recommended

S. cordata is a compact, trailing plant that bears small, white flowers all summer. Cultivars with larger, white or lavender flowers or gold and green variegated foliage are available.

Features: decorative flowers, foliage and habit **Flower color:** white, lavender **Height:** 3–6" **Spread:** 12–20"

Cleome

Cleome

*C*reate a bold and exotic display in your garden with these lovely and unusual flowers.

Growing

Cleome prefers **full sun** but tolerates partial shade. It **adapts to most soils**, though mixing in **organic matter** to help retain water is a good idea. These plants are drought tolerant but perform best when watered regularly. Pinch out the tip of the center stem on young plants to encourage branching and more blooms. Deadhead to prolong blooming and reduce prolific self-seeding.

Tips

Cleome can be planted in groups at the back of a border or in the center of an island bed. These striking plants also make an attractive addition to a large, mixed container.

Recommended

C. hassleriana is a tall, upright plant with strong, supple, thorny stems. The foliage and flowers of this plant have a strong but not unpleasant scent. Flowers are borne in loose, rounded clusters at the ends of the leafy stems. Many cultivars are available.

C. serrulata (Rocky Mountain bee plant) is native to western North America but is rarely available commercially. The thornless dwarf cultivar **'Solo'** is regularly available to be grown from seed and grows 12–18" tall with pink and white flowers.

C. hassleriana 'Royal Queen' (above), *C. hassleriana* (below)

Cleome attracts hummingbirds and provides them with nectar well into fall since the flowers keep on blooming after many other plants have finished for the year.

Also called: spider flower **Features:** attractive, scented foliage and flowers; thorny stems
Flower color: purple, pink, white **Height:** 1–5'
Spread: 12–24"

Coleus

Solenostemon (Coleus)

'Life Lime' (above), *S. scutellarioides* cultivar (below)

From brash yellows, oranges and reds to deep maroon and rose selections, coleus' colors, textures and variations are almost limitless.

Growing

Coleus prefers to grow in **light or partial shade** but tolerates full shade that isn't too dense, or full sun if the plants are watered regularly. The soil should be of **rich to average fertility, humus rich, moist** and **well drained**.

Place the seeds in a refrigerator for one or two days before planting them on the soil surface; the cold temperatures will help break the seeds' dormancy. They need light to germinate. Seedlings are green at first, but leaf variegation will develop as the plants mature.

Tips

The bold, colorful foliage is dramatic when coleus are grouped together as edging plants or in beds, borders or mixed containers. Coleus can also be grown indoors as a houseplant in a bright room.

Pinch off flower buds when they develop; the plants tend to stretch out and become less attractive after they flower.

Recommended

S. scutellarioides (*Coleus blumei* var. *verschaffeltii*) forms a bushy mound of foliage. The leaf edges range from slightly toothed to very ruffled. Leaves are usually multi-colored with shades ranging from pale greenish yellow to deep purple-black. Sun-loving varieties grown from cuttings include 'Alabama Sunset' with spectacular orange, red and yellow leaves; 'Dark Star' with dark, rich, purple-black, scalloped leaves and 'Life Lime' that bears large, gold leaves with occasional splashes of maroon. Many of the dozens of cultivars cannot be started from seed.

Features: brightly colored foliage
Flower color: light purple; grown as a foliage plant **Height:** 6–36" **Spread:** usually equal to height

Fan Flower

Scaevola

Fan flower's intriguing, one-sided flowers add interest to hanging baskets, planters and window boxes.

Growing

Fan flower grows well in **full sun** or **light shade**. The soil should be of **average fertility, moist** and very **well drained**. Water regularly because this plant doesn't like to dry out completely. It does, however, recover quickly from wilting when watered.

Tips

Fan flower is a popular choice for hanging baskets and containers, but it can also be used along the tops of rock walls and in rock gardens, where it will trail down. This plant makes an interesting addition to mixed borders and it can be planted under shrubs, where the long, trailing stems will form an attractive groundcover.

S. aemula (above & below)

Fan flower responds well to pinching and trimming. Frequently pinching the tips or trimming the entire plant back will keep it bushy and blooming.

Recommended

S. aemula forms a mound of foliage from which trailing stems emerge. The fan-shaped flowers come in shades of purple, usually with white bases. The species is rarely grown because there are many improved cultivars.

Given the right conditions, this Australian plant will flower profusely from April through to frost.

Features: unique flowers; trailing habit
Flower color: blue, purple, white
Height: up to 8" **Spread:** up to 4'

Fuchsia

Fuchsia

F. x *hybrida* 'Joy Patmore' (above), F. x *hybrida* cultivar (below)

This beautiful, shade-blooming plant should be grown in every garden.

Growing

Fuchsia grows in **partial or light shade**. It will not tolerate summer heat, and full sun can be too hot for this plant. The soil should be **fertile, moist** and **well drained**. Plant it after the last frost.

Some gardeners who have grown fuchsias in greenhouses over several years have trained the plants to adopt tree forms.

Fuchsia should be deadheaded. Pluck the swollen seedpods from behind the fading petals, or the seeds will ripen and rob the plant of energy it needs for flower production.

Fuchsia blooms on new growth and prefers a plant food high in nitrogen, which encourages new growth.

Tips

Plant upright fuchsias in mixed planters, beds and borders. Pendulous fuchsias are most often used in hanging baskets, but they make attractive additions to planters and rock gardens.

Recommended

Dozens of cultivars of *F.* x *hybrida* are available in both upright and pendulous forms. Cultivars with bronzy red foliage are also available.

Features: colorful, pendent flowers
Flower color: pink, red, orange, purple, purple blue, white; often bicolored **Height:** 6–36"
Spread: 8–36"

Gazania
Gazania

G. *rigens* (above & below)

Few other flowers can rival gazania for adding vivid oranges, reds and yellows to the garden.

Growing

Gazania grows best in **full sun** but tolerates some shade. The soil should be of **poor to average fertility, sandy** and **well drained**. Gazania is drought tolerant and grows best when temperatures climb over 75° F. Flowers may only stay open on sunny days.

Tips

Low-growing gazania makes an excellent groundcover and is also useful on exposed slopes, in mixed containers and as an edging in flowerbeds. It is a wonderful plant for a xeriscape or dry garden design.

Recommended

G. *rigens* forms a low basal rosette of lobed foliage. Large, daisy-like flowers with pointed petals are borne on strong stems above the plant. Many cultivars are available.

This native of southern Africa has very few pests and transplants easily, even when blooming.

Features: colorful flowers **Flower color:** red, orange, yellow, pink, cream **Height:** usually 6–8"; may grow to 12–18" **Spread:** 8–12"

Geranium

Pelargonium

P. 'Frank Headley' (above), *P. peltatum* (below)

Tough, predictable, sun-loving and drought resistant, geraniums have earned their place as flowering favorites in the annual garden. If you are looking for something out of the ordinary, seek out the scented geraniums with their fragrant and often decorative foliage.

Growing

Geraniums prefer **full sun** but will tolerate partial shade, though they may not bloom as profusely. The soil should be **fertile** and **well drained**.

Deadheading is essential to keep geraniums blooming and looking neat.

Tips

Geraniums are very popular annual plants, used in borders, beds, planters, hanging baskets and window boxes.

Geraniums are perennials that are treated as annuals and can be kept indoors over winter in a bright room.

Recommended

P. peltatum (ivy-leaved geranium) has thick, waxy leaves and a trailing habit. Many cultivars are available.

P. species and **cultivars** (scented geraniums, scented pelargoniums) is a large group of geraniums that have scented leaves. The scents are grouped into the categories of rose, mint, citrus, fruit, spice and pungent.

P. zonale (zonal geranium) is a bushy plant with red, pink, purple, orange or white flowers and, frequently, banded or multi-colored foliage. Many cultivars are available.

Ivy-leaved geranium is one of the most beautiful plants to include in a mixed hanging basket.

Features: colorful flowers; decorative or scented foliage; variable habits **Flower color:** red, pink, violet, orange, salmon, white, purple **Height:** 8–24" **Spread:** 6–48"

Impatiens

Impatiens

I. wallerana (above), *I. hawkeri* (below)

Impatiens are the high-wattage darlings of the shade garden, delivering masses of flowers in a wide variety of colors.

Growing

Impatiens do best in **partial or light shade** but tolerate full shade or, if kept moist, full sun. New Guinea impatiens are the best adapted to sunny locations. The soil should be **fertile, humus rich, moist** and **well drained**.

Tips

Impatiens are known for their ability to grow and flower profusely, even in shade. Mass plant them in beds under trees, along shady fences or walls, or in porch planters. They also look lovely in hanging baskets. New Guinea impatiens are grown as much for their variegated leaves as for their flowers.

Recommended

I. hawkeri (New Guinea hybrids, New Guinea impatiens) flowers in shades of red, orange, pink, purple or white. The foliage is often variegated with a yellow stripe down the center of each leaf.

I. wallerana (impatiens, busy Lizzie) flowers in shades of purple, red, burgundy, pink, yellow, salmon, orange, apricot or white, and can be bicolored. Dozens of cultivars are available.

Features: colorful flowers; grows well in shade
Flower color: shades of purple, red, burgundy, pink, yellow, salmon, orange, apricot, white; also bicolored **Height:** 6–36" **Spread:** 12–24"

Million Bells

Calibrachoa

'Terracotta' (above), 'Trailing Pink' (below)

Million bells is charming and, given the right conditions, will bloom continually during the growing season.

Growing

Million bells prefers **full sun**. The soil should be **fertile, moist** and **well drained**. Although it prefers to be watered regularly, million bells is fairly drought resistant once established. The flowers develop hardiness as the weather cools, enabling them to bloom well into fall. Million bells can survive temperatures as low as 20° F.

Tips

A popular choice for planters and hanging baskets, million bells also looks attractive in beds and borders. It grows all summer and needs plenty of room to spread or it will overtake other flowers. Pinch back to keep plants compact. To protect the flower petals from rain, place hanging baskets under the eaves of the house or porch.

Recommended

Calibrachoa hybrids have a dense, trailing habit, and they bear small flowers that look like petunias. Cultivars are available in a wide range of flower colors, including striking, bicolored varieties. The peachy 'Terracotta' looks great paired with intensely colored foliage plants in clay pots.

Calibrachoa flowers close at night and on cloudy days.

Also called: calibrachoa, trailing petunia
Features: colorful flowers; trailing habit
Flower color: pink, purple, yellow, red orange, white, blue **Height:** 6–12" **Spread:** up to 24"

Nemesia

Nemesia

Cute as a button, nemesia has snapdragon-like flowers in a variety of shades. The tall flower spikes of this cool-season annual are often used as long-lasting cut flowers.

Growing

Nemesia prefers **full sun**. The soil should be **average to fertile, slightly acidic**, **moist** and **well drained**. Regular watering will keep these plants blooming through summer.

Tips

Nemesia is a bright and colorful addition to the front of a mixed border or mixed container. It may be slow to start and may fade a bit during the hottest part of summer, but as the weather cools in late summer, nemesia will revive and start flowering once again.

Recommended

N. strumosa, a perennial that is sometimes grown as an annual, forms a bushy mound of bright green foliage. The flowers are carried high above the foliage on tall spikes. The many cultivars offer a variety of solid and bicolored flowers.

'KLM' (above), *N. strumosa* 'Joan Wilder' (below)

Deadhead nemesia to prolong its blooming, and pinch its tips when young to promote a bushy form.

Features: colorful flowers; habit
Flower color: red, blue, purple, pink, white, yellow, orange, bicolored **Height:** 6–24"
Spread: 4–12"

Nierembergia

Nierembergia

'Mont Blanc' (above), *N. hippomanica* var. *violacea* (below)

The flowers of nierembergia float like stars atop fern-like foliage. This plant is lovely for planting under roses and other complementary flowering shrubs.

Growing

Nierembergia grows well in **full sun** or **partial shade**. It does best in the cooler part of the garden where there is protection from the afternoon sun. The soil should be of **average fertility**, **moist** and **well drained**.

Nierembergia is a perennial used as an annual. During a mild year, it may survive winter. Unfortunately, it may also suffer during the heat of summer. If your plant survives winter, take it as a bonus. However, it is often easier to start new plants each year than to overwinter mature plants.

Tips

Use nierembergia as a groundcover, for edging beds and borders, and for rock gardens, rock walls, containers and hanging baskets. It grows best when summers are cool, and it can withstand a light frost.

Recommended

N. frutescens '**Purple Robe**' is a dense, compact plant that bears deep purple flowers with golden eyes.

N. hippomanica var. *violacea* (*N. caerulea*) forms a small mound of foliage. This plant bears delicate, cup-shaped flowers in lavender blue with yellow centers. '**Mont Blanc**' is an All-America Selections (AAS) winner that bears white flowers with yellow centers.

The species name hippomanica *is from the Greek and means 'drive horses crazy.' Whether horses went crazy because they loved to eat it or from actually eating the plant is unclear.*

Features: flowers; habit; foliage
Flower color: blue, purple, white; yellow centers **Height:** 6–12" **Spread:** 6–12"

Pansy
Viola

V. x *wittrockiana* cultivar (above), 'Ultima Morpho' (below)

Pansies are one of the most popular annuals available and for good reason. They're often planted in early spring, long before any other annual, because they tolerate frost like no other. They continue to bloom through spring, summer and fall, requiring little care.

Growing
Pansies prefer **full sun** but tolerate partial shade. The soil should be **fertile, moist** and **well drained**. Pansies do best in cool weather.

Tips
Pansies can be used in beds and borders or mixed with spring-flowering bulbs. They can also be grown in containers. With the varied color combinations available, pansies complement almost every other type of bedding plant.

Plant a second crop of pansies late in summer to refresh tired flowerbeds well into the cool months of fall. Pansies will often reawaken in spring if left to go dormant in fall, allowing for early-spring blooms that aren't afraid of a little late frost.

Recommended
V. x *wittrockiana* is available in a wide variety of solid, patterned, bicolored and multi-colored flowers with face-like markings in every size imaginable. The foliage is bright green and lightly scalloped along the edges.

The more you pick, the more profusely the plants will bloom, so deadhead throughout the summer months.

Also called: viola **Features:** colorful flowers
Flower color: blue, purple, red, orange, yellow, pink, white, multi-colored **Height:** 3–10"
Spread: 6–12"

Petunia
Petunia

Milliflora type 'Fantasy Ivory' (above), Multiflora type (below)

For speedy growth, prolific blooming and ease of care, petunias are hard to beat.

Growing
Petunias prefer **full sun**. The soil should be of **average to rich fertility, light, sandy** and **well drained**. Pinch halfway back in mid-summer to keep plants bushy and to encourage new growth and flowers.

Tips
Use petunias in beds, borders, containers and hanging baskets.

Recommended
P. x *hybrida* is a large group of popular, sun-loving annuals that fall into three categories: **grandifloras** have the largest flowers in the widest range of colors, but they can be damaged by rain; **multifloras** bear more flowers that are smaller and less easily damaged by heavy rain; and the **millifloras** have the smallest flowers in the narrowest range of colors, but this type is the most prolific and least likely to be damaged by heavy rain.

The name Petunia *is derived from* petun, *the Brazilian word for tobacco, which comes from species of the related genus* Nicotiana.

Features: colorful flowers; versatile, upright or cascading plants **Flower color:** pink, purple, red, white, yellow, coral, blue, bicolored **Height:** 6–18" **Spread:** 12–24" or more

Salvia

Salvia

S. splendens (red flowers) and *S. farinacea* (tall purple flowers), *S. viridis* (below)

Salvias should be part of every annual garden. The attractive and varied forms have something to offer every style of garden.

Growing

All salvia plants prefer **full sun** but tolerate light shade. The soil should be **moist** and **well drained** and of **average to rich fertility**, with a lot of **organic matter**.

Tips

Salvias look good grouped in beds and borders and in containers. The flowers are long lasting and make good cut flowers for arrangements.

To keep plants producing flowers, water often and fertilize monthly.

Recommended

S. coccinea (Texas sage) is a bushy, upright plant that bears whorled spikes of white, pink, blue or purple flowers. *S. farinacea* (mealy cup sage, blue sage) has bright blue flowers clustered along stems powdered with silver. Cultivars are available. *S. splendens* (salvia, scarlet sage) is grown for its spikes of bright red, tubular flowers. Recently, cultivars have become available in white, pink, purple and orange. *S. viridis* (*S. horminium;* annual clary sage) is grown for its colorful pink, purple, blue or white bracts, not for its flowers.

There are over 900 species of Salvia.

Also called: sage **Features:** colorful summer flowers; attractive foliage **Flower color:** red, blue, purple, burgundy, pink, orange, salmon, yellow, cream, white, bicolored **Height:** 8"–4' **Spread:** 8"–4'

Snapdragon
Antirrhinum

A. *majus* cultivars (above & below)

Snapdragons are among the most appealing plants. The flower colors are always rich and vibrant, and even the most jaded gardeners are tempted to squeeze open the dragons' mouths.

Growing
Snapdragons prefer **full sun** but tolerate light or partial shade. The soil should be **fertile, rich in organic matter** and **well drained**. These plants prefer a **neutral or alkaline** soil and will not perform as well in acidic soil. Do not cover seeds when sowing because they require light for germination.

Snapdragons are interesting and long lasting in fresh flower arrangements. The buds will continue to mature and open, even after the spike is cut from the plant.

To encourage bushy growth, pinch the tips of the young plants. Cut off the flower spikes as they fade to promote further blooming and to prevent the plant from dying back before the end of the season.

Tips
The height of the variety dictates the best place for it in a border; the shortest varieties work well near the front, and the tallest look good in the center or back. The dwarf and medium-height varieties can also be used in planters. A trailing variety does well in hanging baskets.

Recommended
There are many cultivars of *A. majus* available, generally grouped into three size categories: dwarf, medium and giant.

Snapdragons may self-sow but the hybrids will not come true to type.

Features: entertaining summer flowers
Flower color: white, cream, yellow, orange, red, maroon, pink, purple, bicolored
Height: 6"–4' **Spread:** 6–24"

Sweet Potato Vine

Ipomoea

'Blackie' (above), 'Margarita' (below)

This vigorous, rambling plant with lime green, bruised purple or green, pink and cream variegated leaves can make any gardener look like a genius.

Growing

Grow sweet potato vine in **full sun**. Any type of soil will do, but a **light**, **well-drained** soil of **poor fertility** is preferred.

Tips

Sweet potato vine is a great addition to mixed planters, window boxes and hanging baskets. In a rock garden it will scramble about, and along the top of a retaining wall it will cascade over the edge.

Recommended

I. batatas (sweet potato vine) is a twining climber that is grown for its attractive foliage rather than its flowers. Several cultivars are available.

As a bonus, when you pull up your plant at the end of summer, you can eat any tubers (sweet potatoes) that have formed.

Features: decorative foliage **Flower color:** grown for foliage **Height:** up to 12" **Spread:** up to 10'

Verbena

Verbena

V. x hybrida (above & below)

Verbenas offer butterflies a banquet. Butterfly visitors include tiger swallowtails, silver-spotted skippers, great spangled fritillaries and painted ladies.

Growing

Verbenas grow best in **full sun**. The soil should be **fertile** and very **well drained**. Pinch back young plants for bushy growth.

The Romans, it is said, believed verbena could rekindle the flames of dying love. They named it Herba Veneris, *'plant of Venus.'*

Tips

Use verbenas on rock walls and in beds, borders, rock gardens, containers, hanging baskets and window boxes. They make good substitutes for ivy-leaved geraniums where the sun is hot and where a roof overhang keeps the mildew-prone verbenas dry.

Recommended

V. bonariensis forms a low clump of foliage from which tall, stiff stems bear clusters of small, purple flowers.

V. x hybrida is a bushy plant that may be upright or spreading. It bears clusters of small flowers in a wide range of colors. Cultivars are available.

Also called: garden verbena **Features:** summer flowers **Flower color:** red, pink, purple, blue, yellow, scarlet, silver, peach, white; some with white centers **Height:** 8"–5' **Spread:** 12–36"

Aster

Aster

Purple and pink asters make a nice contrast to the yellow-flowered perennials common in the late-summer garden. You will also have birds, butterflies and bees arriving for a late-summer or fall garden party.

Growing

Asters prefer **full sun** but tolerate partial shade. The soil should be **fertile, moist** and **well drained**. In colder areas, mulch plants in winter to protect from temperature fluctuations. Divide every two or three years to maintain vigor and control spread. Plants will decline rapidly if not divided frequently.

Tips

Plant asters in the middle of borders and in cottage gardens, or naturalize them in wild gardens.

Recommended

Many species and cultivars are available. The following are the most popular species. Check with your local garden center to see what is available in your area.

A. x *frikartii* (Frikart's aster) is a group of mildew-resistant hybrids that bloom nonstop all summer. '**Mönch**' produces purple blue flowers.

A. novae-angliae (Michaelmas daisy, New England aster) is an upright, spreading, clump-forming perennial that bears yellow-centered, purple flowers.

A. novi-belgii (Michaelmas daisy, New York aster) is a dense, upright, clump-forming perennial with purple flowers.

A. novae-angliae (above), *A. novi-belgii* (below)

In early spring, and again in late spring, use hedge shears to cut back bushy, compact plants that don't need staking and to reduce disease problems.

Asters are now becoming popular chrysanthemum substitutes in fall.

Features: late-summer to mid-autumn flowers
Flower color: red, white, blue, purple, pink; often with yellow centers **Height:** 10"–5'
Spread: 18–36" **Hardiness:** zones 3–8

Astilbe

Astilbe

A. *japonica* 'Deutschland' (above)
A. x *grendsii* 'Bressingham Beauty' (below)

Astilbes are beacons in the shade. Their high-impact flowers will brighten any gloomy section of your garden.

In late summer, transplant seedlings found near the parent plant to create plumes of color throughout the garden.

Growing

Astilbes grow best in **light or partial shade** in **fertile, humus-rich, acidic, moist, well-drained** soil. Heavy shade reduces flowering. Astilbes like moist soil in summer, but should not sit in standing water during winter while they are dormant.

Astilbes should be divided every three years or so to maintain plant vigor. Root masses may lift out of the soil as they mature. Add a layer of topsoil and mulch if this occurs, or lift the entire plant and replant in a deeper hole.

Tips

Astilbes can be grown near the edges of bog gardens and ponds and in woodland gardens and shaded borders.

Recommended

A. x *arendsii* (astilbe, false spirea, Arend's astilbe) is a group of hybrids with many available cultivars.

A. chinensis (Chinese astilbe) is a dense, vigorous perennial that tolerates dry soil better than other astilbe species. Many cultivars are available.

A. japonica (Japanese astilbe) is a compact, clump-forming species, rarely grown in favor of its many cultivars.

A. simplicifolia **hybrids** (star astilbe) is a newcomer to the market. These hybrids are mostly compact plants with finely textured foliage and flowers that emerge later in the season. There are many to choose from.

Features: attractive foliage; summer flowers; interesting seedheads **Flower color:** white, pink, purple, peach, red **Height:** 10"–4' **Spread:** 8–36" **Hardiness:** zones 3–8

Beebalm

Monarda

The fragrant flowers are enticing to both our sense of taste and smell but intoxicating to butterflies, bees and all who pass by this plant.

Growing

Beebalm grows well in **full sun, partial shade** or **light shade**. The soil should be of **average fertility, humus rich, moist** and **well drained**. Dry conditions encourage mildew and loss of leaves, so regular watering is a must. Divide every two or three years in spring just as new growth emerges.

In June, cut back some of the stems by half to extend the flowering period and encourage compact growth. Thinning the stems in spring also helps prevent powdery mildew. If mildew strikes after flowering, cut the plants back to 6" to increase air circulation.

M. didyma cultivar (above), *M. didyma* (below)

Tips

Use beebalm beside a stream or pond, or in a lightly shaded, well-watered border. It will spread in moist, fertile soils, but like most mints, the roots are close to the surface and can be removed easily.

The fresh or dried leaves may be used to make a refreshing, minty, citrus-scented tea. Put a handful of leaves in a teapot, pour boiling water over them and let steep for at least five minutes. Sweeten with honey to taste.

Beebalm attracts bees, butterflies and humming-birds to your garden. Avoid using pesticides, which can seriously harm or kill these creatures and which will prevent you from using the plant for culinary or medicinal purposes.

Recommended

M. didyma is a bushy, mounding plant that forms a thick clump of stems with red or pink flowers. Many cultivars are available in varied colors, sizes and levels of mildew resistance, including 'Jacob Cline,' which produces large, scarlet red flowers.

Also called: bergamot, Oswego tea **Features:** fragrant, colorful blossoms **Flower color:** red, pink **Height:** 2–4' **Spread:** 12–24" **Hardiness:** zones 3–8

Bellflower

Campanula

C. medium (above), *C. carpatica* 'White Clips' (below)

Thanks to their wide range of heights and habits, it is possible to put bell-flowers almost anywhere in the garden.

Divide bellflowers every few years, in early spring or late summer, to keep plants vigorous and to prevent them from becoming invasive.

Growing

Bellflowers grow well in **full sun, partial shade** or **light shade**. The soil should be of **average to high fertility** and **well drained**. Mulch to keep roots cool and moist in summer and protected in winter, particularly if snow cover is inconsistent. Deadhead to prolong blooming.

Tips

Plant upright and mounding bellflowers in borders and in cottage gardens. Use low, spreading and trailing bellflowers in rock gardens and on rock walls. You can also edge beds with the low-growing varieties.

Recommended

C. carpatica (Carpathian bellflower, Carpathian harebell) is a spreading, mounding perennial that bears blue, white or purple flowers in summer. Several cultivars are available.

C. glomerata (clustered bellflower) forms a clump of upright stems and bears clusters of purple, blue or white flowers most of summer.

C. medium (Canterbury bells) is an upright plant with narrow leaves and bell-shaped flowers with recurved edges. Dwarf cultivars and double forms are available.

C. persicifolia (peach-leaved bellflower) is an upright perennial that bears white, blue or purple flowers from early summer to mid-summer.

Features: spring, summer or autumn flowers; varied growing habits **Flower color:** blue, white, purple, pink **Height:** 4–36" **Spread:** 12–24" **Hardiness:** zones 2–7

Black-Eyed Susan

Rudbeckia

R. fulgida with purple coneflower (above)

Black-eyed Susan is a tough, low maintenance, long-lived perennial. Plant it wherever you want a casual look. Black-eyed Susan looks great planted in drifts.

Growing

Black-eyed Susan grows well in **full sun** or **partial shade**. The soil should be of **average fertility** and **well drained**. Several *Rudbeckia* species are touted as 'claybusters' because they tolerate fairly heavy clay soils. Established plants are drought tolerant, but regular watering is best. Divide in spring or fall, every three to five years.

Tips

Include these native plants in wildflower and natural gardens, beds and borders. Pinching the plants in June will result in shorter, bushier stands.

Recommended

R. fulgida is an upright, spreading plant bearing orange-yellow flowers with brown centers. Var. *sullivantii* 'Goldsturm' bears large, bright, golden yellow flowers.

R. laciniata (cutleaf coneflower) forms a large, open clump. The yellow flowers have green centers. 'Goldquelle' has bright yellow, double flowers.

Features: bright flowers; attractive foliage; easy to grow **Flower color:** yellow, orange, red, with centers typically brown or green **Height:** 2–6' **Spread:** 18–36" **Hardiness:** zones 3–8

Bleeding Heart
Dicentra

D. eximia (above), *D. spectabilis* (below)

Every garden should have a bleeding heart. Tucked away in a shady spot, this lovely plant appears in spring and fills the garden with fresh promise.

Growing

Bleeding hearts prefer **light shade** but tolerate partial or full shade. The soil should be **humus rich, moist** and **well drained**. These plants die back in very dry summers but revive in autumn or the following spring. Bleeding hearts must remain moist while blooming to prolong the flowering period. Regular watering will keep the flowers coming until mid-summer.

D. exima and *D. spectabilis* rarely need dividing. *D. formosa* can be divided every three years or so.

Tips

Bleeding hearts can be naturalized in a woodland garden or grown in a border or rock garden. They make excellent early-season specimen plants and do well near ponds or streams.

All bleeding hearts contain toxic alkaloids, and some people develop allergic skin reactions from contact with these plants.

Recommended

D. eximia (fringed bleeding heart) forms a loose, mounded clump of lacy, fern-like foliage and bears pink or white flowers in spring and sporadically over summer.

D. formosa (western bleeding heart) is a low-growing, wide-spreading plant with pink flowers that fade to white as they mature. The most drought tolerant of the bleeding hearts, it is the most likely to continue flowering all summer.

D. spectabilis (common bleeding heart, Japanese bleeding heart) forms a large, elegant mound that bears flowers with white inner petals and pink outer petals. Several cultivars are available.

Features: spring and summer flowers; attractive foliage **Flower color:** pink, white, red, purple **Height:** 8–36" **Spread:** 12–24" **Hardiness:** zones 2–8

Brunnera
Brunnera

Brunnera is often recommended as the best substitute or accompaniment to hostas for its vigor, tiny blue flowers, tolerance of shade and richly variegated cultivars.

Growing

Brunnera prefers **light shade** but tolerates morning sun with consistent moisture. The soil should be of **average fertility, humus rich, moist** and **well drained**. The species and its cultivars do not tolerate drought. Cut back faded foliage mid-season to produce a flush of new growth. Divide in spring when the center of the clump begins to die out.

Tips

Brunnera makes a great addition to a woodland or shaded garden. Its low, bushy habit makes it useful as a groundcover or as an addition to a shaded border.

Recommended

B. macrophylla forms a mound of soft, heart-shaped leaves and produces loose clusters of blue flowers all spring. **'Dawson's White'** ('Variegata') has large leaves with irregular creamy patches. **'Hadspen Cream'** has leaves with creamy margins. **'Jack Frost'** is a newer cultivar that produces silvery leaves with green veins, and **'Langtrees'** has mostly green leaves with silvery marks. Grow variegated plants in light or full shade to avoid scorched leaves.

'Jack Frost' (above), 'Dawson's White' (below)

Named after Swiss botanist Samuel Brunner (1790–1844), brunnera is related to borage and forget-me-nots. Its previous botanical name, Anchusa myosotidiflora, *translates as 'flowers that look like* Myosotis *(forget-me-nots).'*

This reliable plant rarely suffers from any problems.

Also called: Siberian bugloss
Features: coarsely textured foliage; flowers; form **Flower color:** blue **Height:** 12–18"
Spread: 18–24" **Hardiness:** zones 3–8

Butterfly Weed
Asclepias

A. incarnata (above), A. tuberosa (below)

Native to North America, butterfly weed is a major food source for the monarch butterfly and will attract butterflies to your garden.

Be careful not to pick off or destroy the green-and-black-striped caterpillars that feed on these plants, as they will eventually turn into beautiful monarch butterflies.

Growing
Butterfly weed prefers **full sun**. The soil should be **fertile**, **moist** and **well drained**, though *A. tuberosa* is drought tolerant. To propagate, remove the seedlings that will sprout up around the base of these plants. The deep taproot makes division very difficult.

Deadhead to encourage a second blooming.

Tips
Use *A. tuberosa* in meadow plantings and borders, on dry banks, in neglected areas and in wildflower, cottage and butterfly gardens. Use *A. incarnata* in moist borders and in bog, pondside or streamside plantings.

Butterfly weeds are slow to start in spring.

Recommended
A. incarnata (swamp milkweed) bears clusters of pink, white or light purple flowers in late spring or early summer. Although it naturally grows in moist areas, it appreciates a well-drained soil in the garden. Many cultivars are available in a variety of colors and forms.

A. tuberosa (butterfly weed) forms a clump of upright, leafy stems. It bears clusters of orange flowers from midsummer to early fall. A variety of cultivars exist, bearing flowers in shades of scarlet, gold, orange, pink and bicolored.

Also called: milkweed, pleurisy root
Features: flowers; form **Flower color:** orange, scarlet, gold, yellow, white, red, pink, light purple, bicolored **Height:** 18–36" **Spread:** 12–24" **Hardiness:** zones 3–9

Candytuft

Iberis

Candytuft is invaluable for bringing soft, soothing color to semi-shady portions of the yard and garden.

Growing

Candytuft prefers to grow in **full sun** or **partial shade**. Partial shade is best if it gets very hot in your garden. Like many species in the mustard family, candytuft dislikes heat; blooming will often slow down or decrease in July and August. The soil should be of **poor or average fertility, well drained** and have a **neutral or alkaline** pH.

Deadheading when the seeds begin to form will keep candytuft blooming, but do let some plants go to seed to guarantee repeat performances.

Tips

This informal plant can be used on rock walls, in mixed containers or as edging for beds.

Recommended

I. sempervirens is a spreading evergreen, bearing clusters of tiny, white flowers in spring. Many cultivars are available in varied sizes, forms and habits, including **'Autumn Snow,'** which bears white flowers in spring and fall.

I. sempervirens (above & below)

If you arrive home after dusk on a spring night, the white flowers of candytuft will welcome you with a lovely glow in the moonlight.

Features: profuse flowering habit
Flower color: white **Height:** 6–12"
Spread: 8" or more
Hardiness: zones 3–8

Catmint

Nepeta

'Walker's Low' (above), *N. x faassenii* (below)

The real workhorses of the garden bed, catmints offer season-long blooms on sturdy, trouble-free plants.

Growing

These plants prefer **full sun** or **partial shade**. Grow them in **well-drained** soil of **average fertility**; the growth tends to flop in rich soil. Plant in spring; divide in spring or fall when they look overgrown and dense.

In June, pinch the tips to delay flowering and to make the plants more compact.

Tips

Catmint forms upright, spreading clumps. Plant it in herb gardens, perennial beds, rock gardens, cottage gardens with roses or as edging along borders and pathways.

Recommended

N. x faassenii bears blue or purple flowers. Cultivars with gray-green foliage and pink, white, light purple or lavender blue flowers are available, as well as low-growing cultivars. A fine example of this is **'Walker's Low,'** which has gray-green foliage and bears lavender blue flowers.

N. **'Six Hills Giant'** bears deep lavender blue flowers.

Like all members of the mint family, catmint has square stems.

Features: aromatic foliage; attractive flowers; easy to grow **Flower color:** blue, purple, white, pink **Height:** 18–36" **Spread:** 12–24" **Hardiness:** zones 3–8

Columbine

Aquilegia

*D*elicate and beautiful columbines add a touch of simple elegance to any garden. Blooming from spring through to mid-summer, these long-lasting flowers herald the passing of cool spring weather and the arrival of summer.

Growing

Columbines grow well in **light shade** or **partial shade**. They prefer soil that is **fertile, moist** and **well drained**, but they adapt to most soil conditions. Division is not required but can be done to propagate desirable plants. Divided plants may take a while to recover because columbines dislike having their roots disturbed.

Tips

Use columbines in rock gardens, formal or casual borders and naturalized or woodland gardens. Place them where other plants can fill in to hide the foliage as columbines die back over summer.

If leaf miners are a problem, cut the foliage back once flowering is complete and new foliage will fill in.

Recommended

A. canadensis (wild columbine, Canada columbine) is a native plant that is common in woodlands and fields. It bears yellow flowers with red spurs.

A. x *hybrida* (*A.* x *cultorum;* hybrid columbine) forms mounds of delicate foliage and has exceptional flowers. Many hybrids have been developed with showy flowers in a wide range of colors.

A. vulgaris 'Nora Barlow' (above)
A. x hybrida 'McKana Giants' (below)

A. vulgaris (European columbine, common columbine) has been used to develop many hybrids and cultivars with flowers in a variety of colors and forms, including double-flowered cultivars that look like frilly dahlias.

Columbines self-seed but are not invasive. Each year a few new seedlings may turn up near the parent plant and can be transplanted.

Features: spring and summer flowers; attractive foliage
Flower color: red, yellow, pink, purple, blue, white; color of spurs often differs from that of the petals
Height: 18–36" **Spread:** 12–24" **Hardiness:** zones 3–8

Coral Bells

Heuchera

H. micrantha (above), H. sanguinea (below)

From soft yellow greens and oranges to midnight purples and silvery, dappled maroons, coral bells offer a great variety of foliage options for a perennial garden with partial shade.

Growing

Coral bells grow best in **light or partial shade**. The foliage colors can bleach out in full sun, and plants grow leggy in full shade. The soil should be of **average to rich fertility, humus rich, neutral to alkaline, moist and well drained**.

Good air circulation is essential. Deadhead to prolong the bloom. Every two or three years, coral bells should be dug up and the oldest, woodiest roots and stems removed. Plants may be divided at this time, if desired, then replanted with the crown at or just above soil level.

Tips

Use coral bells as edging plants, in clusters and woodland gardens or as groundcovers in low-traffic areas. Combine different foliage types for an interesting display.

Recommended

H. americana is a mound-forming perennial with heart-shaped marbled foliage and bronze veins when young that mature to a deep green. Cultivars have been developed for their attractive and variable foliage.

H. micrantha is another mounding species that grows more than twice the size of the other species. It produces gray-green foliage and white flowers. The cultivars are more commonly grown, including the ever-popular 'Palace Purple.' It is a compact cultivar with deep purple leaves and white flowers on burgundy stems.

H. sanguinea (red coral bells) produces a mound of small, rounded leaves. The leaves are often deep green but occasionally they're mottled with silver markings or variegated. Tiny, red flowers emerge through the foliage on tall, wiry stems. Many cultivars are available in varied forms, leaf colors and patterns.

Also called: heuchera, alum root **Features:** very decorative foliage; spring or summer flowers **Flower color:** red, pink, white, yellow, purple; plant also grown for foliage **Height:** 12–30" **Spread:** 6–18" **Hardiness:** zones 3–8

Cranesbill

Geranium

G. *sanguineum* cultivars (above & below)

There is a type of geranium that suits every garden, thanks to the beauty and diversity of this hardy plant.

Growing

Cranesbill dislikes hot weather but grows well in **full sun, partial shade** or **light shade** and prefers soil of **average fertility** and **good drainage**. G. *renardii* prefers a poor, well-drained soil. Divide in spring.

Tips

These long-flowering plants are great in a border; they fill in the spaces between shrubs and other larger plants, and keep the weeds down. They can be included in rock gardens and woodland gardens or mass planted as groundcovers.

Recommended

G. 'Brookside' is a clump-forming, drought-tolerant cranesbill with finely cut leaves and deep blue to violet blue flowers. (Zones 4–8)

G. 'Johnson's Blue' forms a spreading mat of foliage topped with bright blue flowers over a long period in summer. (Zones 3–8)

G. *macrorrhizum* (bigroot geranium, scented cranesbill) forms a spreading mound of fragrant foliage and bears flowers in various shades of pink. Cultivars are available.

G. *sanguineum* (bloodred cranesbill, bloody cranesbill) forms a dense, mounding clump and bears bright magenta flowers. Many cultivars are available. (Zones 3–8)

Also called: cranesbill geranium
Features: summer flowers; attractive, sometimes fragrant foliage **Flower color:** white, red, pink, purple, blue **Height:** 4–18"
Spread: 12–24" **Hardiness:** zones 2–8

Daylily
Hemerocallis

'Dewey Roquemore' (above), 'Bonanza' (below)

The daylily's adaptability and durability combined with its variety in color, blooming period, size and texture explain this perennial's popularity.

Growing
Daylilies grow in any light from **full sun to full shade**. The deeper the shade, the fewer flowers that will be produced. The soil should be **fertile, moist** and **well drained**, but these plants adapt to most conditions and are hard to kill once established. Divide every two or three years to keep plants vigorous and to propagate them. They can, however, be left indefinitely without dividing.

Tips
Plant daylilies alone, or group them in borders, on banks and in ditches to control erosion. They can be naturalized in woodland or meadow gardens. Small varieties are nice in planters.

Deadhead to prolong the blooming period. Be careful when deadheading purple-flowered daylilies because the sap can stain fingers and clothes.

Recommended
Daylilies come in an almost infinite number of forms, sizes and colors in a range of species, cultivars, hybrids and recurrent blooming varieties. Contact your local garden center or daylily grower to find out what's available and most suitable for your garden.

Features: spring and summer flowers; grass-like foliage
Flower color: every color except blue and pure white
Height: 1–4' **Spread:** 1–4' **Hardiness:** zones 2–8

False Indigo
Baptisia

B. australis 'Purple Smoke' (above), B. australis (below)

False indigo can be considered a three-season plant. It produce spikes of beautiful pea-blossom flowers in spring and interesting brown 'pea pods' in summer and fall. Throughout the growing season it provides a lovely foliage backdrop for other plants.

Growing
False indigo prefers **full sun** but tolerates partial shade. Too much shade results in lank growth that causes the plant to split and fall. The soil should be of **average or poor fertility, sandy** and **well drained**. False indigo is happy to remain in the same place for a long time and often resents being divided. Staking may be required if your plant is not getting enough sun. To prevent having to worry about staking or moving the plant, place it in the sun and give it a lot of space to spread.

Tips
False indigo can be used in an informal border or cottage-type garden. Use it in a natural planting, on a slope or in any well-drained, sunny spot. When first planted, false indigo may not look too impressive, but once established it is long-lived, attractive and dependable.

Recommended
B. australis is an upright or somewhat spreading, clump-forming plant that bears spikes of purple blue flowers. **'Purple Smoke'** bears lighter purple flowers.

Features: unusual flowers; drought tolerant
Flower color: purple blue, white **Height:** 3–5'
Spread: 2–4' **Hardiness:** zones 3–9

Gayfeather
Liatris

L. spicata 'Kobold' (above), *L. spicata* (below)

Gayfeather is an outstanding cut flower with fuzzy, spiked blossoms above grass-like foliage. This native wildflower is an excellent plant for attracting butterflies to the garden.

Growing

Gayfeather prefers **full sun**. The soil should be of **average fertility, sandy** and **humus rich**. Water well during the growing season, but don't allow the plant to stand in water during cool weather. Mulch during summer to prevent moisture loss. Gayfeather is quite drought tolerant once established.

Trim the spent flower spikes to promote a longer blooming period and to keep gayfeather looking tidy. Spikes can be left on the plant toward the end of the flowering season for winter interest. Gayfeather will self-seed, but seedlings may not be identical to the parent plant.

Tips

Use gayfeather in borders and meadow plantings where the tall flowering spikes can create a striking contrast with other perennials and shrubs. Plant in a location that has good drainage to avoid root rot in winter. Gayfeather grows well in planters.

Recommended

L. spicata is a clump-forming, erect plant with pinkish purple or white flowers. Several cultivars are available.

The spikes make excellent, long-lasting cut flowers. Plants can be divided every three to five years when the clump starts to look crowded.

Also called: blazing star **Features:** summer flowers; grass-like foliage **Flower color:** purple, white **Height:** 18–36" **Spread:** 18–24" **Hardiness:** zones 3–9

Goat's Beard

Aruncus

Despite its imposing size, goat's beard has a soft and delicate appearance with its divided foliage and large, plumy, cream flowers.

Growing

Goat's beard prefers **partial to full shade**. If planted in deep shade, it bears fewer blooms. It tolerates some full sun as long as the soil is kept evenly moist and is protected from the afternoon sun. The soil should be **fertile, moist** and **humus rich**.

Divide in spring or autumn. Use a sharp knife or an ax to cut the dense root mass into pieces. Fortunately, this plant rarely needs dividing.

Tips

These plants look very natural when grown near the sunny entrance or edge of a woodland garden, in a native plant garden or in a large island planting. They may also be used in a border or alongside a stream or pond.

Recommended

*A. **aethusifolius*** (dwarf Korean goat's beard) forms a low-growing, compact mound and bears branched spikes of loosely held, cream flowers.

*A. **dioicus*** (giant goat's beard, common goat's beard) forms a large, bushy, shrub-like perennial with large plumes of creamy white flowers. Several cultivars are available.

A. dioicus (above & below)

Male and female flowers are produced on separate plants. Male flowers are full and fuzzy, and female flowers are more pendulous.

Bees and butterflies simply adore the feathery plumes throughout the summer months.

Features: early- to mid-summer blooms; shrub-like habit; attractive foliage and seedheads **Flower color:** cream, white **Height:** 6"–6' **Spread:** 12"–4' **Hardiness:** zones 2–8

Hollyhock
Alcea

A. rosea (above & below)

Tips

Because they are so tall, hollyhocks look best at the back of a border or in the center of an island bed. If placed up against a fence they will get some support from the fence. In any windy location they will need to be staked. Hollyhocks may be grown shorter and bushier with smaller flowers if the main stem is pinched out early in the season. These shorter flower stems are less likely to be broken by the wind and therefore can be left unstaked.

Old-fashioned hollyhocks typically have single flowers and grow much taller than newer hybrids but are more disease resistant. Growing them as biennials and removing them after they flower is a good way to keep rust at bay.

Recommended

A. rosea forms a rosette of leaves with tall flowering stalks bearing ruffled single or double blooms.

A. rugosa (Russian hollyhock) is similar to *A. rosea* but is more resistant to hollyhock rust. It bears pale yellow to orangy yellow single flowers.

A. rosea was originally grown as a food plant; the young leaves were added to salads.

Nothing says 'storybook charm' like hollyhocks against a picket fence or stone wall, gently waving in warm summer breezes, tall and proud.

Growing

Hollyhocks prefer to grow in **full sun** but tolerate partial shade. The soil should be of **average to rich** fertility and **well drained**. New daughter plants that develop around the base of the mature plant may be divided off in order to propagate fancy or desirable specimens. They don't always come true to type from seed, so this may be the only way to get more of a plant that is particularly attractive.

Features: tall, architectural form; colorful flowers **Flower color:** yellow, white, apricot, pink, red, purple or reddish black **Height:** 5–8' **Spread:** 24" **Hardiness:** zones 2–8

Hosta

Hosta

H. sieboldiana 'Elegans' (above)

Plant breeders are always looking for new variations in hosta foliage. Swirls, stripes, puckers and ribs enhance the leaves' various sizes, shapes and colors. Sun-loving hostas have recently become the new rage for gardens.

Growing

Hostas prefer **light or partial shade** but will grow in full shade. Morning sun is preferable to afternoon sun in partial shade situations. The soil should ideally be **fertile, moist** and **well drained**, but most soils are tolerated. Hostas are fairly drought tolerant, especially if given a mulch to help retain moisture. Division is not required but can be done every few years in spring or summer to propagate new plants.

Tips

Hostas make wonderful woodland plants and look very attractive when combined with ferns and other fine-textured plants. They are also good plants for a mixed border, particularly when used to hide the ugly, leggy lower stems and branches of some shrubs. Hostas' dense growth and thick, shade-providing leaves allow them to suppress weeds.

Recommended

Hostas have been subjected to a great deal of crossbreeding and hybridizing, resulting in hundreds of cultivars. Visit your local garden center or get a mail-order catalog to find out what's available.

Also called: plantain lily **Features:** decorative foliage; summer and autumn flowers **Flower color:** white, purple; grown mainly for foliage **Height:** 4–36" **Spread:** 6"–6' **Hardiness:** zones 2–8

Iris
Iris

I. sibirica (above), *I.* x *germanica* 'Stepping Out' (below)

Irises are steeped in history and lore. Many say the range in flower colors of bearded irises approximates that of a rainbow.

Growing
Irises prefer **full sun** but tolerate very light or dappled shade. The soil should be of **average fertility** and **well drained**. Japanese iris and Siberian iris prefer a moist but still well-drained soil.

Divide in late summer or early autumn. When dividing bearded iris rhizomes, replant with the flat side of the foliage fan facing the garden. Deadhead irises to keep them tidy. Cut the foliage back in spring or fall along with your other perennials.

Tips
Irises are popular border plants; Japanese iris and Siberian iris are also useful alongside streams or ponds. Dwarf cultivars are attractive in rock gardens.

Wash your hands after handling irises because they can cause severe internal irritation if ingested. Do not plant them close to children's play areas.

Recommended
Among the most popular of the many species and hybrids is the bearded iris, often a hybrid of *I.* x *germanica.* It has the widest range of flower colors but is susceptible to the iris borer. Several irises are not susceptible, including Japanese iris (*I. ensata*), dwarf bearded iris (*I. pumila*) and Siberian iris (*I. sibirica*).

Features: spring, summer and sometimes autumn flowers; attractive foliage **Flower color:** many shades of pink, red, purple, blue, white, brown, yellow **Height:** 8"–4' **Spread:** 6"–4' **Hardiness:** zones 2–8

Joe-Pye Weed

Eupatorium

These architectural plants add volume and stature to the garden and put on a good show of late-season flowers.

Growing

Joe-Pye weed prefers **full sun to partial shade**. The soil should be **fertile** and **moist**, though wet soils are tolerated.

Tips

These plants can be used in a moist border or near a pond or other water feature. The tall types work well at the back of a border or in the center of a bed where they can create a backdrop for lower-growing plants.

Recommended

E. coelestinum (hardy ageratum) is a bushy, upright plant that bears clusters of flossy, light blue to lavender flowers.

E. maculatum (*E. purpureum*) is a huge plant that bears clusters of purple flowers at the ends of wine purple stems. '**Gateway**' is a slightly shorter plant with much larger, rose pink flower clusters and reddish stems.

E. rugosum (*Ageratina altissima;* boneset, white snakeroot) forms a bushy, mounding clump of foliage and bears clusters of white flowers. '**Chocolate**' is a slightly smaller plant with dark purple leaves that mature to dark green.

E. rugosum (above), *E. maculatum* (below)

Joe-Pye weed provides a punch of color in a fall garden and attracts butterflies.

Also called: boneset, snakeroot **Features:** late-summer to fall flowers; foliage; habit **Flower color:** white, purple, blue, pink, lavender **Height:** 2–10' **Spread:** 1½–4' **Hardiness:** zones 3–9

Lady's Mantle
Alchemilla

A. mollis (above & below)

Few other perennials are as captivating as lady's mantle when it's dappled with morning dew. The fine-haired leaves capture water, creating pearly drops that cling to the edges of the leaves.

Alchemists in the Middle Ages thought the dew captured in the center of the leaf could change lead into gold.

Growing
Lady's mantle plants prefer **light or partial shade** with protection from the afternoon sun. They dislike hot locations, and excessive sun will scorch the leaves. The soil should be **fertile**, **humus rich**, **moist** and **well drained**. These plants are drought resistant once established. Deadhead to keep the plants tidy and possibly encourage a second flush of flowers in late summer or fall.

Tips
Lady's mantle is ideal for grouping under trees in woodland gardens and along border edges. It softens the bright colors of other plants. It is also attractive in containers.

Recommended
A. mollis forms a mound of soft, rounded foliage and produces sprays of frothy-looking, yellowish green flowers in early summer.

Features: round, fuzzy leaves; tiny flowers
Flower color: yellow, green **Height:** 8–18"
Spread: 20–24" **Hardiness:** zones 3–8

Lamb's Ears

Stachys

The soft, fuzzy leaves of lamb's ears give this perennial its common name. The silvery foliage is a beautiful contrast to bold-colored plants that tower above; it softens hard lines and surfaces.

Growing

Lamb's ears grows best in **full sun**. The soil should be of **poor or average fertility** and **well drained**. The leaves can rot in humid weather if the soil is poorly drained. Remove spent flower spikes to keep the plant looking neat.

Tips

Lamb's ears makes a great groundcover in a new garden where the soil has not yet been amended. It can be used to edge borders and

S. byzantina (above & below)

pathways because it provides a soft, silvery backdrop for more vibrant colors in the border. For a silvery accent, plant a small group of lamb's ears in a border.

Recommended

S. byzantina forms a mat of thick, woolly rosettes of leaves. Pinkish purple flowers bloom all summer. There are many cultivars that offer a variety of foliage colors, sizes and flowers, including 'Helene von Stein' which produces fuzzy leaves twice as large as other species or cultivars.

Like many plants in the mint family, lamb's ears has medicinal properties. It not only feels soft but may actually encourage healing.

Also called: lamb's tails, lamb's tongues **Features:** soft, fuzzy, silver foliage **Flower color:** pink, purple **Height:** 6–18" **Spread:** 18–24" **Hardiness:** zones 3–8

Ligularia
Ligularia

Ligularias are stunning plants, but only in areas where they receive adequate moisture and protection from afternoon sun. The foliage and flowers are truly unforgettable.

Growing

Ligularias should be grown in **light shade** or **partial shade** with protection from the afternoon sun. They will thrive in full sun but only with consistently moist soil. The soil should be of **average fertility**, **humus rich** and **moist**.

Tips

Plant ligularias alongside a pond or stream. They can also be used in a well-watered border or bog garden, or naturalized in a moist meadow or woodland garden.

Recommended

L. dentata (bigleaf ligularia, golden groundsel) forms a clump of rounded, heart-shaped leaves and bears clusters of orange-yellow, daisy-like flowers. Cultivars are available in varied sizes and colors.

L. stenocephala (narrow-spiked ligularia) has toothed foliage and bears bright yellow flowers on dark, purple-green spikes.

L. stenocephala 'The Rocket' (above), *L. dentata* (below)

The foliage can wilt in hot sun, even in moist soil. The leaves will revive overnight, but it is best to plant ligularia in a cool, shaded place in the garden.

Features: flowers; ornate foliage
Flower color: yellow, orange **Height:** 3–6'
Spread: 2–5' **Hardiness:** zones 3–9

Monkshood

Aconitum

*T*he wonderful blooms of this back-of-the-border beauty provide much-appreciated color late in the growing season, often lasting well into October.

Growing

Monkshood grows best in **light or partial shade**. It will grow in any **moist** soil but prefers a **rich** soil with a lot of **organic matter** worked in. Monkshood prefers not to be divided because it may be slow to re-establish. If division is desired to increase the number of plants, it should be done in late fall after blooming or in early spring. When dividing or transplanting monkshood, never plant the crown at a depth lower than where it was previously growing. Burying the crown any deeper will cause it to rot and the plant to die.

Tall monkshoods may need to be staked. Peony hoops or tomato cages inserted around young plants will be hidden as the plants fill in.

Tips

Monkshood is perfect for cool, boggy locations along streams or next to ponds. It makes a tall, elegant addition to woodland gardens in combination with lower-growing plants. Do not plant monkshood near tree roots because it cannot compete with trees.

It will do poorly when the weather gets hot, particularly if conditions do not cool down at night. Mulch the roots to keep it cool; keep it well watered; and trim back faded foliage in summer to encourage new growth to fill in when cooler fall

A. napellus (above & below)

weather arrives. Do not cut back too hard or the plant will fail to flower.

Recommended

A. x *cammarum* (Cammarum hybrids) contains several of the more popular hybrid cultivars. '**Bicolor**' (bicolor monkshood) bears blue and white, helmet-shaped flowers. '**Bressingham Spire**' bears dark purple blue flowers on strong spikes.

A. charmichaelii (azure monkshood) forms a low mound of basal leaves from which the flower spikes emerge, clothed in purple or blue flowers. Cultivars are available in taller selections that are far more tolerant to heat.

A. napellus (common monkshood) is an erect plant that forms a basal mound of finely divided foliage. It bears dark purple blue flowers.

Features: tall, colorful flower spikes; habit
Flower color: purple, blue, white, bicolored
Height: 3–6' **Spread:** 12–18"
Hardiness: zones 3–8

Peony

Paeonia

P. *lactiflora* 'Shimmering Velvet' (above)
P. *lactiflora* cultivars (below)

Once the fleeting, but magnificent, peony flower display is done, the foliage remains stellar throughout the growing season.

Growing

Peonies prefer **full sun** but tolerate some shade. The planting site should be well prepared with **fertile, humus-rich, moist, well-drained** soil with a lot of compost. Mulch peonies lightly with compost in spring. Too much fertilizer, particularly nitrogen, causes floppy growth and retards blooming. Division is not required but can be done in fall to propagate plants. Deadhead to keep plants looking tidy.

Tips

Peonies look great in a border combined with other early bloomers. They may be underplanted with bulbs—when the other plants die down by mid-summer, the emerging peony foliage will hide the dying foliage. Avoid planting peonies under trees, where they will have to compete for moisture and nutrients.

Tubers planted too shallowly or too deeply will not flower. The buds or eyes on the tuber should be 1–2" below the soil surface.

Place wire tomato or peony cages around the plants in early spring to support the heavy flowers. The foliage will grow into the wires and hide the cage.

Recommended

There are hundreds of peonies available. Cultivars come in a wide range of colors, may have single or double flowers and may or may not be fragrant. Visit your local garden center to check for availability.

Features: spring and early-summer flowers; attractive foliage **Flower color:** white, cream white, yellow, pink, red, purple **Height:** 24–32" **Spread:** 24–32" **Hardiness:** zones 2–8

Phlox

Phlox

Phlox comes in many shapes and sizes, from low creepers to bushy border plants, with flowering periods falling anywhere between early spring and mid-autumn.

Growing

P. maculata and *P. paniculata* prefer **full sun**; *P. stolonifera* prefers **light to partial shade** but tolerates heavy shade, and *P. subulata* prefers **full sun to partial shade**. All like **fertile, humus-rich, moist, well-drained** soil. Divide in spring or autumn.

Tips

Low-growing species are useful in rock gardens or at the front of borders. Taller phloxes may be used in the middle of borders and are particularly effective if planted in groups.

Recommended

P. maculata (early phlox, garden phlox, wild sweet William) forms an upright clump of hairy stems and narrow leaves that are sometimes spotted with red. Pink, purple or white flowers are borne in conical clusters.

P. paniculata (garden phlox, summer phlox) is an upright plant. The many cultivars vary in size and flower color.

P. stolonifera (creeping phlox) is a low, spreading plant that bears flowers in several shades of purple.

P. subulata (moss phlox, moss pink) is very low growing and bears flowers in various colors. The foliage is evergreen.

P. paniculata cultivars (above & below)

Phlox comes in many forms, from low-growing creepers to tall, clump-forming uprights. The many species can be found in varied climates from dry, exposed mountainsides to moist, sheltered woodlands.

Features: spring, summer or autumn flowers
Flower color: white, blue, purple, orange, pink, red **Height:** 2"–4' **Spread:** 12–36"
Hardiness: zones 2–8

Purple Coneflower
Echinacea

E. purpurea (above & below)

Purple coneflower is a native wildflower renowned for its medicinal value and the visual delight it creates in the landscape, having pinkish purple petals that encircle spiky, orange centers.

Growing

Purple coneflower grows well in **full sun** or very **light shade**. It tolerates any well-drained soil but prefers an **average to rich** soil. The thick taproots make this plant drought resistant, but it prefers to have regular water. Divide every four years or so in spring or fall.

Deadhead early in the season to prolong flowering. Later you may wish to leave the flowerheads in place to self-seed and provide winter interest. Pinch plants back or thin out the stems in early June to encourage bushy growth that is less prone to mildew. This will also encourage a later but longer blooming period.

Tips

Plant purple coneflowers in meadow gardens and informal borders, either in groups or as single specimens. Purple coneflower combines well with ornamental grasses and blue- or yellow-flowered perennials and shrubs.

Recommended

E. purpurea is an upright plant covered in prickly hairs. It bears pinkish purple flowers with conical, orangy centers, and it has several cultivars: '**Magnus,**' the 1998 Perennial Plant of the Year, has purple petals that stand out from the central cone; '**Razzmatazz**' has bright pink petals and a pom-pom-like flower form; and '**White Swan**' has white petals.

Also called: coneflower, echinacea Features: mid-summer to fall flowers; persistent seedheads
Flower color: purple, pink, white; rusty orange centers
Height: 2–5' Spread: 12–24" Hardiness: zones 3–8

Queen of the Prairie

Filipendula

For an impressive, informal, vertical accent and showy clusters of fluffy, fragrant flowers, queen-of-the-prairie plants are second to none.

Growing

Queen of the prairie prefers **partial or light shade** but tolerates full sun if the soil remains sufficiently moist. The soil should be **fertile, deep, humus rich** and **moist**, except in the case of *F. vulgaris*, which prefers dry soil. Divide in spring or fall.

Tips

Most queen-of-the-prairie plants are excellent for bog gardens or wet sites. Grow them alongside streams or in moist meadows. Queen of the prairie may also be grown in the back of a border, as long as it is kept well watered. Grow *F. vulgaris* if you can't provide the moisture needed by the other species.

Recommended

F. rubra (queen of the prairie) forms a large, spreading clump and bears clusters of fragrant, pink flowers. Cultivars are available.

F. ulmaria (queen-of-the-meadow) forms a mounding clump and bears creamy white flowers in large clusters. Cultivars are available.

F. vulgaris (dropwort, meadowsweet) is a low-growing species that bears clusters of fragrant, creamy white flowers. Cultivars with double or pink flowers or variegated foliage are available.

F. ulmaria 'Variegata' (above), *F. ulmaria* (below)

Deadhead queen of the prairie if you so desire, but the faded seedheads are quite attractive when left in place.

Features: late-spring or summer flowers; attractive foliage **Flower color:** white, cream, pink, red **Height:** 2–8' **Spread:** 1½–4' **Hardiness:** zones 3–8

Russian Sage

Perovskia

P. *atriplicifolia* (above), 'Filigran' (below)

Russian sage offers four-season interest in the garden: soft, gray-green leaves on light gray stems in spring; fuzzy, violet blue flowers in summer; and silvery white stems in autumn that last until late winter.

Growing

Russian sage prefers **full sun**. The soil should be **poor to moderately fertile** and **well drained**. Too much water and nitrogen will cause this plant's growth to flop, so do not plant it next to heavy feeders. In spring, when new growth appears low on the branches, or in autumn, cut the plant back hard to about 6–12" to encourage vigorous, bushy growth.

Tips

The silvery foliage and blue flowers work well with other plants in the back of a mixed border and soften the appearance of daylilies. Russian sage can also create a soft screen in a natural garden or on a dry bank.

Recommended

P. atriplicifolia is a loose, upright plant with silvery white, finely divided foliage. The small, lavender blue flowers are loosely held on silvery, branched stems. Many cultivars are available, including **'Filigran,'** which has delicate foliage and an upright habit; **'Lace,'** a shorter cultivar; and **'Little Spire,'** which is half the size of the species but identical in every other way.

Russian sage blossoms make a lovely addition to fresh bouquets and dried-flower arrangements.

Features: mid-summer to autumn flowers; attractive habit; fragrant gray-green foliage
Flower color: blue, purple **Height:** 3–4'
Spread: 3–4' **Hardiness:** zones 4–9

Sedum
Sedum

Some 300 to 500 species of sedum are distributed throughout the Northern Hemisphere. Many sedums are grown for their foliage, which can range in color from steel gray-blue and green to red and burgundy.

Growing

Sedums prefer **full sun** but tolerate partial shade. The soil should be of **average fertility**, very **well drained** and **neutral to alkaline**. Divide in spring when needed.

Tips

Low-growing sedums make wonderful groundcovers and additions to rock gardens or rock walls. They also edge beds and borders beautifully. Taller sedums give a lovely late-season display in a bed or border.

Recommended

S. acre (gold moss stonecrop) is a low-growing, wide-spreading plant that bears small, yellow-green flowers.

S. kamtschaticum is a low-growing carpet of scalloped, green foliage, covered with bright yellow, starry flowers.

S. spectabile (showy stonecrop) is an upright species with pink flowers. Cultivars are available.

S. spurium (two-row stonecrop) forms a low, wide mat of foliage with deep pink or white flowers. Many cultivars are available and are often grown for their colorful foliage.

S. spurium cultivars (above), *S. spectabile* (below)

Light pinching of upright species and hybrids in early summer encourages compact, bushy growth, but it also can delay flowering.

Also called: stonecrop **Features:** summer to fall flowers; decorative, fleshy foliage
Flower color: yellow, white, red, pink; also grown for foliage **Height:** 2–24" **Spread:** 12–24" or more
Hardiness: zones 2–8

Tickseed

Coreopsis

C. rosea (above), *C. grandiflora* (below)

This popular perennial brings warm and sunny hues to naturalized plantings with their bright, daisy-like blooms all summer long.

Growing

Tickseed plants prefer **full sun** and will often become stretched and floppy in partial shade. The soil should be of **average to rich fertility, light** and **well drained**. Poor soil is tolerated but with somewhat reduced flowering. Good drainage is the most important factor for these drought-tolerant plants.

Tips

Try tickseed in front of a rustic wooden fence or repeating in clusters in a bed of perennials. Tickseed provides a beautiful color combination when planted next to plants with deep purple foliage or flowers. Effective in naturalized meadow plantings, tickseed can also be used in informal beds and borders where it will flower all season if deadheaded regularly. These plants also produce lovely cut flowers.

Tickseed plants can be blown over or have their stems broken during heavy rain or high winds. The fine foliage isn't dense enough to hide tomato or peony cages, so insert twiggy branches for the seedlings to grow between for support. In very windy spots, it is best to use the dwarf forms of tickseed.

Recommended

C. auriculata (mouse-eared tickseed) will steadily creep outward without becoming invasive. Cultivars are available that bear orange-yellow flowers in late spring.

C. grandiflora (large-flowered coreopsis, tickseed) forms a clump of foliage and bears bright, golden yellow flowers over a long period in mid- and late summer. Cultivars are grown more often than the species and have received the prestigious AAS award.

C. rosea (pink tickseed) is an unusual species with pink flowers.

C. verticillata (thread-leaf coreopsis) is a mound-forming plant with attractive, finely divided foliage. A variety of cultivars offer different forms and sizes.

Features: bright flowers; long-blooming habit
Flower color: yellow, red, pink, orange, brown
Height: 18"–4' **Spread:** up to 18" **Hardiness:** zones 3–8

Arborvitae

Thuja

T. occidentalis 'Little Gem' (above), *T. occidentalis* (below)

Arborvitae are rot resistant, durable and long lived, earning quiet admiration from gardeners everywhere.

Growing

Arborvitae prefer **full sun** but tolerate light to partial shade. The soil should be of **average fertility, moist** and **well drained.** These plants enjoy humidity and perform best in a location sheltered from wind, especially in winter when the foliage can easily dry out, giving the plant a rather brown, drab appearance.

Tips

Large varieties of arborvitae make excellent specimen trees, and smaller cultivars can be used in foundation plantings, shrub borders and as formal or informal hedges.

Recommended

T. occidentalis (eastern arborvitae, eastern white cedar) is a narrow, pyramidal tree with scale-like evergreen needles. There are dozens of cultivars available, including shrubby, dwarf varieties, varieties with yellow foliage and smaller upright varieties. (Zones 2–7; cultivars may be less cold hardy)

T. plicata (western arborvitae, western redcedar) is a narrowly pyramidal evergreen tree that grows quickly, resists deer browsing and maintains good foliage color all winter. Several cultivars are available, including dwarf varieties and a yellow and green variegated variety. (Zones 5–9)

Also called: cedar **Features:** foliage; bark; form **Habit:** small to large, evergreen shrub or tree **Height:** 2–50' **Spread:** 2–20' **Hardiness:** zones 2–8

Ash
Fraxinus

F. americana 'Autumn Blaze' (above)
F. pennsylvanica (below)

Ash is often planted in traffic medians and parking lots, and it will provide shade by the poolside.

*T*he ash is not flashy, but it has many solid qualities. Its fall colors are gently glowing and luminous, a harmonious complement to the vivid oranges and reds of other autumn showoffs.

Growing
Ash grows best in **full sun**. The soil should be **fertile** and **moist** with a lot of room for root growth. These trees tolerate drought, poor soil, salt and pollution.

Tips
Ash is a quick-growing shade tree. It grows well in the moist soil alongside streams and ponds or in low-lying areas that never seem to dry out.

Recommended
F. americana (white ash) is a large, wide-spreading tree. Fall color ranges from yellow to purple. Cultivars are available in varied forms, in sizes smaller than the species.

F. mandshurica (Manchurian ash) is more compact in form and very hardy. Seedless selections are available.

F. nigra (black ash, swamp ash) grows very tall and wide. Seedless cultivars are available that offer great fall color and longer periods in leaf.

F. pennsylvanica (green ash, red ash) is an irregular, spreading tree. It grows very tall and equally as wide. Its foliage turns yellow, sometimes with orange or red, in fall. Seedless selections are available.

Features: fall color; fast growth habit
Habit: upright or spreading, deciduous tree
Height: 50–80' **Spread:** 25–80'
Hardiness: zones 3–8

Barberry

Berberis

The variations available in plant size, foliage color and fruit make barberry a real workhorse of the plant world.

Growing

Barberry develops the best fall color when grown in **full sun**, but it tolerates partial shade. Any **well-drained** soil is suitable. This plant tolerates drought and urban conditions but suffers in poorly drained, wet soil.

B. thunbergii 'Crimson Pygmy' (above), *B. thunbergii* 'Atropurpurea' (below)

Tips

Large barberry plants make great hedges with formidable prickles. Barberry can also be included in shrub and mixed borders. Small cultivars can be grown in rock gardens, in raised beds and along rock walls.

Recommended

B. koreana (Korean barberry) is a larger species that adapts well to dry sites throughout the state.

B. thunbergii (Japanese barberry) is a dense shrub with a broad, rounded habit. The foliage is bright green and turns variable shades of orange, red or purple in fall. Yellow, spring flowers are followed by glossy red fruit later in summer. Many cultivars have been developed for their variable foliage color, including shades of purple, yellow and variegated varieties.

Features: foliage; flowers; fruit
Flower color: yellow **Habit:** prickly, deciduous shrub **Height:** 12"–5' **Spread:** 12"–5'
Hardiness: zones 4–8

Beech

Fagus

F. sylvatica 'Pendula' (above), *F. sylvatica* (below)

The aristocrat of large, shade trees, the majestic beech is attractive at any age, from its big, bold, beautiful youth through to its slow, craggy decline.

Growing

Beeches grow equally well in **full sun** or **partial shade**. The soil should be of **average fertility**, **loamy** and **well drained**, though almost all well-drained soils are tolerated.

American beech doesn't like having its roots disturbed and should be transplanted only when very young. European beech transplants easily and is more tolerant of varied soil conditions than is American beech.

Tips

Beeches make excellent specimens. They are also used as shade trees and in woodland gardens. These trees need a lot of space, but the European beech's adaptability to pruning makes it a reasonable choice in a small garden.

Recommended

F. grandifolia (American beech) is a broad-canopied tree native to most of eastern North America.

F. sylvatica (European beech) is a spectacular, broad tree with a number of interesting cultivars. Several are small enough to use in the home garden, from narrow columnar and weeping varieties to those with purple or yellow leaves or pink, white and green variegated foliage.

Features: foliage; bark; habit; fall color; fruit **Habit:** large, oval, deciduous shade tree **Height:** 30–80' **Spread:** 10–65' **Hardiness:** zones 4–8

Birch

Betula

It seems like birch trees have graced the Iowa landscape forever. Although birch has struggled in times of drought, it has earned a respected status throughout the region.

Growing

Birches grow well in **full sun, partial shade** or **light shade**. The soil should be of **average to rich fertility, well drained** and **moist**. Many birch species naturally grow in wet areas, such as alongside streams, but they don't like permanently soggy conditions.

Tips

Often used as a specimen tree, a birch's small leaves and open canopy provide light shade that allows perennials, annuals or lawns to flourish beneath.

Recommended

B. nigra (river birch, black birch) has shaggy, cinnamon brown bark that flakes off in sheets when it is young but thickens and becomes ridged as it matures. This fast-growing tree has bright green leaves with silvery white undersides. This species is one of the most disease resistant and also resists bronze birch borer. Cultivars are available in varied sizes, including a dwarf form.

B. populifolia 'Whitespire' (*B. platyphylla* var. *japonica*

B. populifolia 'Whitespire' (above), *B. nigra* (below)

'Whitespire') has a distinctive, spire-like habit, with chalky white bark and glossy green leaves that turn yellow in fall. It is resistant to bronze birch borer and is only moderately susceptible to leaf miners.

Rough-textured, black, diamond-shaped patterns are commonly found on the bark of older trees.

Features: foliage; habit; bark; winter and early-spring catkins **Habit:** open, deciduous tree **Height:** 10–90' **Spread:** 10–60' **Hardiness:** zones 2–8

Boxwood

Buxus

B. microphylla var. *koreana* (above), *B. sempervirens* (below)

Boxwoods are versatile evergreens. They can be pruned to form neat hedges, geometric shapes or fanciful creatures. When allowed to grow naturally, boxwoods form attractive, rounded mounds.

Growing

Boxwoods prefer to grow in **partial shade,** but they tolerate full sun if kept well watered. The soil should be **fertile, moist** and **well drained.** Mulching will benefit these shrubs.

Tips

These shrubs make excellent background plants in mixed borders.

Boxwood foliage contains **toxic** compounds that can cause severe digestive upset and possibly death if ingested.

Recommended

B. microphylla (littleleaf boxwood) is quite pest resistant and hardy in zones 6–8. The foliage tends to lose its green in winter. *B. m.* var. *koreana* is hardy to zone 4.

B. sempervirens (common boxwood) is a larger species with foliage that stays green in winter. Cultivars are available with interesting features such as compact or dwarf growth, variegated foliage and pendulous branches. (Zones 5–8)

Several cultivars developed from crossing *B. m.* var. *koreana* and *B. sempervirens* exhibit good hardiness and pest resistance, and they have attractive year-round foliage.

Also called: box **Features:** foliage; slow, even growth **Habit:** dense, rounded, evergreen shrub **Height:** 3–15' **Spread:** equal to height **Hardiness:** zones 4–8

Burning Bush

Euonymus

urning bush makes a fine specimen and works well as a background or border plant for stunning fall color and interesting bark. The wintercreeper euonymus, with its interesting leaf colorings and plant habits, also has many uses.

Growing

Burning bush prefers **full sun** but tolerates light or partial shade. Soil of **average to rich fertility** is preferable but any **moist, well-drained** soil will do.

Tips

E. alatus can be grown in a shrub or mixed border, as a specimen, in a naturalistic garden or as a hedge. Dwarf cultivars can be used to create informal hedges. *E. fortunei* can be grown as a shrub in borders or as a hedge. It is an excellent substitute for the more demanding boxwood. The trailing habit also makes it useful as a groundcover or climber.

Recommended

E. alatus (burning bush, winged euonymus) is an attractive, open, mounding, deciduous shrub with vivid red fall foliage. Winter interest is provided by the corky ridges, or wings, that grow on the stems and branches. Cultivars are available. (Zones 3–8)

E. fortunei (wintercreeper euonymus) as a species is rarely grown,

E. alatus (above & below)

owing to the wide variety of attractive cultivars that are available. These can be prostrate, climbing or mounding evergreens, often with striking variegated foliage. Winter protection is necessary. (Zones 4–8)

Features: foliage; corky stems *(E. alatus)*; habit
Habit: deciduous and evergreen shrub, small tree, groundcover or climber **Height:** 1–6' **Spread:** 2–6'
Hardiness: zones 2–8

Chokeberry

Aronia

A. melanocarpa 'Autumn Magic' (above), *A. melanocarpa* (below)

Chokeberry is a versatile and tough shrub that displays fall color that few others can match.

Growing

Chokecherry grows well in **full sun** or **partial shade**, but the best flowering and fruiting occur in full sun. It grows best in **well-drained** soil of **average fertility** but adapts to most soils and tolerates wet, dry or poor soil.

Up to one-third of the stems, preferably the older ones, can be pruned out annually once flowering is finished.

Tips

Chokecherry is useful in a shrub or mixed border. It also makes an interesting, low-maintenance specimen plant. Left to its own devices, chokecherry will naturalize to cover a fairly large area.

Recommended

A. arbutifolia (*Photinia floribunda;* red chokeberry) is an upright shrub that bears white flowers in late spring, followed by bright red, waxy fruit in fall. 'Brilliantissima' has brilliant red fall foliage.

A. melanocarpa (*A. prunifolia, Photinia melanocarpa;* black chokeberry) is an upright, suckering shrub that bears white flowers in late spring and early summer, followed by dark fruit that ripens in fall and persists through winter. The foliage turns bright red to purplish red in fall.

Chokeberry fruit requires a lot of sweetening to make it palatable. Its bitterness has an aesthetic advantage, however; the birds avoid eating it, so the red or black fruit persists from the time it appears in mid-fall right through winter.

Features: flowers; fruit; fall foliage
Habit: suckering, deciduous shrub
Flower color: white **Height:** 3–10'
Spread: 3–10' **Hardiness:** zones 3–8

Cotoneaster
Cotoneaster

C. apiculatus (above), *C. acutifolius* (below)

With its diverse sizes, shapes, flowers, fruit and foliage, cotoneaster is so versatile that it borders on being overused.

Growing
Cotoneasters grow well in **full sun** or **partial shade**. The soil should be of **average fertility** and **well drained**.

Tips
Cotoneasters can be included in shrubs or mixed borders. Low spreaders work well as groundcover, and shrubby species can be used to form hedges. Larger species are grown as small specimen trees and some low growers are grafted onto standards and grown as small, weeping trees.

Recommended
There are many cotoneasters to choose from. *C. acutifolius* (Peking cotoneaster) is frequently used for hedging. *C. adpressus* (creeping cotoneaster) is a low-growing groundcover species and *C. apiculatus* (cranberry cotoneaster) forms a mound of arching, tangled branches. *C. lucidus* (hedge cotoneaster) is also used for hedging because of its dense growth habit, dark, lustrous leaves and great fall color. These are just a few possibilities; your local garden center can help you find a suitable one for your garden.

Features: foliage; early-summer flowers; persistent fruit; variety of forms
Habit: evergreen or deciduous groundcover, shrub or small tree
Flower color: white **Height:** 1–10'
Spread: 3–7' **Hardiness:** zones 3–8

Dogwood
Cornus

C. *florida* (above), C. *kousa* var. *chinensis* (below)

Whether your garden is wet, dry, sunny or shaded, there is a dogwood for almost every condition. Stem color, leaf variegation, fall color, growth habit, soil adaptability and hardiness are all positive attributes to be found in the dogwoods.

Growing
Dogwoods grow equally well in **full sun, light shade** or **partial shade**, with a slight preference for light shade. The soil should be of **average to high fertility, high in organic matter, neutral or slightly acidic** and **well drained.**

Tips
Use dogwood shrubs along the edge of a woodland, in a shrub

or mixed border, alongside the house, or near a pond, water feature or patio. They look best in groups rather than as single specimens.

Recommended
C. alba (red-twig dogwood, Tartarian dogwood) and *C. sericea* (*C. stolonifera*; red-osier dogwood) are grown for the bright red stems that provide winter interest. Cultivars are available with stems in varied shades of red, orange and yellow. Fall foliage color can also be attractive.

C. alternifolia (pagoda dogwood) can be grown as a large, multi-stemmed shrub or as a small, single-stemmed tree. The branches have an attractive layered look. Clusters of small, white flowers appear in early summer. Cultivars are available with yellow variegated foliage. (Zones 3–8)

C. florida (flowering dogwood) is usually grown as a small tree, featuring horizontally layered branches and showy pink or white blossoms that appear in late spring. Many equally beautiful cultivars are available. (Zones 5–9)

C. kousa (Kousa dogwood) is grown for its flowers, fruit, fall color and interesting bark. This species is more resistant to leaf blight and other problems than *C. florida*. The white-bracted, early-summer flowers are followed by bright red fruit. The foliage turns red and purple in fall. Many varieties and cultivars are available, including varied forms and variegated foliage. (Zones 5–9)

Features: late-spring to early-summer flowers; fall foliage; stem color; fruit; habit
Habit: deciduous, large shrub or small tree
Flower color: white, pink **Height:** 5–15'
Spread: 5–20' **Hardiness:** zones 2–8

False Cypress
Chamaecyparis

Conifer shoppers are blessed with a marvelous selection of false cypresses that offer color, size, shape and growth habits not available in most other evergreens.

Growing

False cypresses prefer **partial shade** with protection from excessive sun and wind. The soil should be **fertile, moist, neutral to acidic** and **well drained**. Alkaline soils are tolerated. In shaded areas, growth may be sparse or thin.

Tips

Tree varieties of false cypresses are used as specimen plants and for hedging. The dwarf and slow-growing cultivars are used in borders, rock gardens or as bonsai. False cypress shrubs can be grown near the house or as evergreen specimens in large containers.

Recommended

C. nootkatensis (yellow-cedar, Nootka false cypress) is a tall tree species rarely grown in favor of the cultivars. 'Pendula' has a very open habit and even more pendulous foliage than the species.

C. obtusa (Hinoki false cypress) is a large, evergreen tree with foliage arranged in fan-like sprays. The many cultivars on the market offer very dwarf forms, gold-tipped foliage and varied habits.

C. pisifera (Japanese false cypress, Sawara cypress) is another tall tree form. The cultivars are far more popular than the species, including very dwarf forms, varied habits and golden foliage.

C. pisifera cultivar (above), *C. nootkatensis* (below)

The oils in the foliage of false cypresses may be irritating to sensitive skin.

Features: foliage; habit; cones **Habit:** narrow, pyramidal, evergreen tree or shrub **Height:** 3–100' **Spread:** 5–36' **Hardiness:** zones 4–8

Fir
Abies

A. concolor 'Candicans' (above & below)

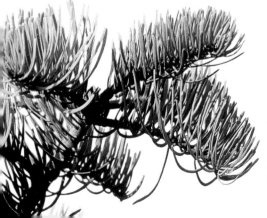

For year-round color and appeal, fir trees are stately and make fine substitutes for more common coniferous trees.

Growing
Firs usually prefer **full sun** but tolerate partial shade. The soil should be **rich, moist, neutral to acidic** and **well drained**. Firs prefer a sheltered site out of the wind. Generally, they do not tolerate polluted city conditions.

Tips
Firs make impressive specimen trees in large areas. Dwarf cultivars can be included in shrub borders or planted as specimens.

Recommended
A. concolor (white fir) is a large, pyramidal to conical tree. The needles have a whitish coating that gives the tree a hazy blue appearance. Cultivars with even whiter needles are also available.

A. concolor *tolerates pollution, heat and drought better than other* Abies *species.*

Features: foliage; cones **Habit:** narrow, pyramidal or columnar, evergreen tree **Height:** 10–70' **Spread:** 15–25' **Hardiness:** zones 3–7

Flowering Crabapple
Malus

Pure white through deep pink flowers, heights between 5' and 25' with similar spreads, tolerance of winter's extreme cold and summer's baking heat, plus tiny fruit—from green to candy apple red—that persists through winter. What more could anyone ask from a tree?

Growing

Flowering crabapples prefer **full sun** but tolerate partial shade. The soil should be of **average to rich fertility, moist** and **well drained**. These trees tolerate damp soil.

Many pests overwinter in the fruit, leaves or soil at the base of the tree. Clearing away their winter shelter helps keep populations under control. To prevent the spread of crabapple pests and diseases, clean up all the leaves and fruit that fall off the tree.

Tips

Flowering crabapples make excellent specimen plants. Many varieties are quite small, so there is one to suit almost any size of garden. The flexible, young branches of flowering crabapples make them good choices for creating espalier specimens along a wall or fence.

Recommended

There are hundreds of flowering crabapples available. When choosing a species, variety or cultivar, the most important attributes to look for are disease resistance and size at maturity. Ask for information about new, resistant cultivars at your local nursery or garden center.

Features: spring flowers; late-season and winter fruit; fall foliage; habit; bark **Habit:** rounded, mounded or spreading, small to medium, deciduous tree **Flower color:** white, pink **Height:** 5–25' **Spread:** 6–20' **Hardiness:** zones 2–8

Flowering Quince
Chaenomeles

C. speciosa 'Texas Scarlet' (above & below)

They may be considered old-fashioned by some, but flowering quinces are simply magnificent in bloom.

Growing

Flowering quinces grow equally well in **full sun** or **partial shade** but bear fewer flowers and fruit in shaded locations. The soil should be of **average fertility, moist** and **well drained**. Slightly acidic soil is preferred. These shrubs tolerate pollution.

Tips

Flowering quinces can be included in shrub or mixed borders. They look attractive grown against walls. Their spiny habit also makes them useful for barriers. Use them along the edge of a woodland or in naturalistic gardens. The dark bark stands out well in winter.

Leaf drop in mid- to late summer may be caused by leaf spot. Draw attention away from the plant with later-flowering perennials or shrubs.

Recommended

C. japonica (Japanese flowering quince) is a spreading shrub that bears orange or red flowers that appear in early to mid-spring, followed by small, fragrant, greenish yellow fruit. This species is not as commonly grown as *C. speciosa* and its cultivars.

C. speciosa (common flowering quince) is a large, tangled, spreading shrub. Red flowers emerge in spring and are followed by fragrant, greenish yellow fruit. Many cultivars are available, including 'Texas Scarlet,' which bears many red flowers over a fairly long period on plants about half the size of the species. 'Toyo-Nishiki' is more upright than the species, with white, pink and red flowers that all appear on the same plant.

Features: spring flowers; fruit; spines
Habit: spreading, deciduous shrub with spiny branches **Flower color:** orange, red, white, pink **Height:** 2–10' **Spread:** 2–15'
Hardiness: zones: 5–9

Ginkgo
Ginkgo

Be patient with ginkgo. Its gawky, irregularly angular youth will eventually pass to reveal a spectacular mature specimen.

Growing

Ginkgo prefers **full sun**. The soil should be **fertile, sandy** and **well drained**, but this tree adapts to most conditions. It is also tolerant of urban conditions and cold weather.

Tips

Although its growth is very slow, ginkgo eventually becomes a large tree that is best suited as a specimen tree in parks and large gardens. It can be used as a street tree.

If you buy an unnamed plant, be sure it has been propagated from cuttings. Seed-grown trees may prove to be female, and the stinky fruit is not something you want dropping all over your lawn, driveway or sidewalk.

Recommended

G. biloba is variable in habit. The uniquely fan-shaped leaves can turn an attractive shade of yellow in fall. Several cultivars are available.

G. biloba (above & below)

Also called: maidenhair tree
Features: summer and fall foliage; habit; fruit; bark Habit: conical in youth, variable with age; deciduous tree Height: 40–100'
Spread: 10–100' Hardiness: zones 3–8

Hackberry
Celtis

Hackberry tolerates any and all conditions in Iowa, and it responds with brawn and grace.

Growing

Hackberry prefers **full sun**. It adapts to a variety of soil types including poor and dry soils. **Deep soils** with **adequate moisture** and **drainage** are best.

Tips

Hackberry is an ideal shade tree specimen for expansive, windy areas. It grows as tall as it does wide and requires a lot of space to grow to its full size without conflict.

Recommended

C. occidentalis is a medium to large tree with a rounded head. The head is made up of arching branches covered in simple but classic foliage. Inconspicuous flowers emerge in spring, followed by dark red or purple, pea-sized fruits in fall.

Hackberry has everything to offer but asks little in return. It provides cool shade in the hot summer months and magnificent foliar color in fall.

C. occidentalis (above & below)

Hackberry is often used in landscape planting as a substitute for elm.

Also called: American hackberry, common hackberry, nettle tree **Features:** form; hardiness; colorful berries; tolerant of poor conditions **Habit:** high-headed, oval, deciduous tree **Height:** 30–50' **Spread:** 30–50' **Hardiness:** zones 2–8

Hawthorn

Crataegus

Hawthorns are uncommonly beautiful trees with a generous spring show of beautiful, miniature, rose-like blossoms, persistent glossy red fruit and good fall color.

Growing

Hawthorns grow equally well in **full sun** or **partial shade**. They adapt to any **well-drained** soil and tolerate urban conditions.

Tips

Hawthorns can be grown as specimen plants for informal landscapes and gardens. They require little care and are ideal flowering ornamentals for small spaces.

These trees are small enough to include in most gardens. With their stiff, 2" long, sharp thorns, however, a hawthorn might not be a good selection if there are children about.

Recommended

C. crus-galli 'Inermis' (thornless cockspur hawthorn) is a small, drought-tolerant tree that bears white flowers followed by red, persistent fruit and orange fall color. (Zones 4–8)

C. douglasii (black hawthorn) is a medium-sized, thorny, low-headed tree with gray bark and reddish twigs. It bears clusters of white flowers followed by black fruit. Cultivars are available and are grown more frequently than the species.

C. laevigata (*C. oxycantha;* English hawthorn) is a low-branching, rounded tree with zigzag layers of thorny branches. It bears white or pink flowers followed by

C. laevigata 'Paul's Scarlet' (above & below)

red fruit in late summer. Many cultivars are available. (Zones 4–8)

C. x *mordenensis* is a small ornamental tree with double white or pink flowers followed by sparse red berries. A few cultivars are available.

C. phaenopyrum (*C. cordata;* Washington hawthorn) is an oval to rounded, thorny tree that bears white flowers and persistent, shiny red fruit in fall. The glossy green foliage turns red and orange in fall.

Features: late-spring or early-summer flowers; fruit; foliage; thorny branches **Habit:** rounded, deciduous tree, often with a zigzagged, layered branch pattern and twisted trunk **Flower color:** white, pink **Height:** 15–30' **Spread:** 10–20' **Hardiness:** zones 3–8

Hemlock

Tsuga

T. canadensis 'Jeddeloh' (above), *T. canadensis* (below)

Many people would agree that eastern hemlock is one of the most beautiful, graceful evergreen trees in the world. Its movement, grace and soft appearance make it easy to place in the landscape.

Growing

Hemlock generally grows well in any light from **full sun to full shade**. The soil should be **humus rich, moist** and **well drained**. Hemlock is drought sensitive and grows best in cool, moist conditions.

It is also sensitive to air pollution and suffers salt damage, so keep it away from roadways.

Tips

This elegant tree, with its delicate needles, is one of the most beautiful evergreens to use as a specimen tree. Hemlock can be pruned to keep it within bounds or shaped to form a hedge. The many dwarf forms are useful in smaller gardens.

Recommended

T. canadensis (eastern hemlock, Canadian hemlock) is a graceful, narrowly pyramidal tree. Many cultivars are available, including groundcover, pendulous and dwarf forms.

Features: foliage; habit; cones **Habit:** pyramidal or columnar, evergreen tree or shrub **Height:** 18"–80' **Spread:** 18"–35' **Hardiness:** zones 3–8

Honeylocust
Gleditsia

G. t. var. inermis 'Sunburst' (above), *G. triacanthos var. inermis* (below)

Thornless honeylocust remains a popular tree for lawn and street plantings. The brilliant, deep yellow fall color is wonderful to behold.

Growing
Thornless honeylocust prefers **full sun**. The soil should be **fertile** and **well drained**. This tree adapts to most soil types.

Tips
Use honeylocust and its numerous cultivars as street trees or specimen trees in larger yards. Smaller selections are more appropriate for smaller yards.

Recommended
G. triacanthos var. *inermis* is a spreading, rounded to flat-topped, thornless tree with inconspicuous flowers and sometimes long, pea-like pods that persist into fall. The autumn color is a warm golden yellow. Many cultivars are available, including compact and weeping varieties and varieties with bright yellow spring foliage.

This adaptable, quick-growing tree provides very light shade, making it a good choice for lawns.

Features: summer and fall foliage; habit
Habit: rounded, spreading, deciduous tree
Height: 15–100' **Spread:** 15–70'
Hardiness: zones 4–8

Hornbeam

Carpinus

C. caroliniana (above), C. betulus 'Fastigiata' (below)

The leaves of the hornbeam remain a bright, fresh green through the oppressive humidity of summer.

Hornbeams may not be spectacular, but they do look good year-round. They are slow growing and, therefore, useful for small yards.

Growing

Hornbeams prefer **full sun** but tolerate partial or light shade. The soil should be **average to fertile** and **well drained**.

Tips

These small- to medium-sized trees can be used as specimens or shade trees in smaller gardens or can be pruned to form hedges. The narrow, upright cultivars are often used to create barriers and windbreaks.

Recommended

C. betulus (European hornbeam) is a pyramidal to rounded tree. The foliage turns bright yellow or orange in fall. Many cultivars are available, including narrow upright and weeping selections.

C. caroliniana (American hornbeam, ironwood, musclewood, bluebeech) is a small, slow-growing tree that tolerates shade and city conditions. The foliage turns yellow to red or purple in fall.

Features: habit; fall color
Habit: pyramidal, deciduous tree
Height: 10–65' **Spread:** 10–50'
Hardiness: zones 4–8

Hydrangea
Hydrangea

ydrangeas have many attractive qualities, including showy, often long-lasting flowers and glossy green leaves, some of which turn beautiful colors in fall.

Growing

Hydrangeas grow well in **full sun** or **partial shade** but some species tolerate full shade. Shade or partial shade will reduce leaf and flower scorch in hotter gardens. The soil should be of **average to high fertility, humus rich, moist** and **well drained**. These plants perform best in cool, moist conditions.

Tips

Hydrangeas come in many forms and have many uses in the landscape. They can be included in shrub or mixed borders, used as specimens or informal barriers and planted in groups or containers.

Recommended

H. arborescens (smooth hydrangea) is a rounded shrub that flowers well, even in shady conditions. This species is rarely grown in favor of the cultivars that bear large clusters of showy white blossoms. (Zones 3–9)

H. macrophylla (bigleaf hydrangea) is a large-flowered species that repeats blooms almost all summer long. The blooms are often pink in alkaline soils but display a blue cast in acidic soil. Newer cultivars are now available in a variety of colors and more than a few are hardy to zone 4, including ENDLESS SUMMER, which bears pink to blue clustered blossoms. (Zones 4–8)

H. paniculata 'Grandiflora' (above & below)

H. paniculata (panicle hydrangea) is a spreading to upright, large shrub or small tree that bears white flowers from late summer to early fall. 'Grandiflora' (Peegee hydrangea) is a commonly available cultivar.

H. quercifolia (oakleaf hydrangea) is a mound-forming shrub with attractive, cinnamon brown, exfoliating bark. Its large leaves are lobed like an oak's and turn bronze to bright red in fall. It has conical clusters of sterile and fertile flowers. (Zones 4–8)

Features: flowers; habit; foliage; bark
Habit: deciduous; mounding or spreading shrub or tree **Flower color:** white, pink **Height:** 3–8'
Spread: 3–8' **Hardiness:** zones 3–8

Juniper
Juniperus

J. sabina 'Broadmoor' (above), *J. horizontalis* 'Blue Prince' (below)

With the various junipers available, from low-creeping plants to upright pyramidal forms, there are endless uses for them in the garden.

Growing

Junipers prefer **full sun** but tolerate light shade. Ideally the soil should be of **average fertility** and **well drained**, but these plants tolerate most conditions.

Wear long sleeves and gloves when handling junipers—the prickly foliage gives some gardeners a rash. Juniper 'berries' are poisonous if eaten in large quantities.

Tips

Junipers can make prickly barriers and hedges, and they can be used in borders, as specimens or in groups. The larger species can be used to form windbreaks, and the low-growing species can be used in rock gardens and as groundcovers.

Recommended

Junipers vary from species to species and often within a species. Cultivars are available for all species and may differ significantly from the species. *J. chinensis* (Chinese juniper) is a conical tree or spreading shrub. *J. communis* (common juniper) is a low-growing, spreading species. *J. horizontalis* (creeping juniper) is a prostrate, creeping groundcover. *J. sabina* (savin juniper) is a low-growing, groundcover species. *J. scopulorum* (Rocky Mountain juniper) can be upright, rounded, weeping or spreading. *J. squamata* (singleseed juniper) forms a prostrate or low, spreading shrub or a small, upright tree.

Features: foliage; variety of color, size and habit
Habit: conical or columnar tree, rounded or spreading shrub, prostrate groundcover; evergreen
Height: 4"–16' **Spread:** 2–8' **Hardiness:** zones 2–8

Kentucky Coffee Tree

Gymnocladus

This stately tree may not be inspiring to some, but it is loved by others for its unique form and habit, as no two trees are exactly alike.

Growing

Kentucky coffee tree grows best in **full sun**. It prefers **fertile, moist, well-drained** soil but adapts to a range of conditions. This tree tolerates alkaline soil, drought and urban conditions.

Pruning is rarely required. Remove dead, diseased or damaged growth as needed, and do any necessary formative pruning in fall or spring.

Tips

Kentucky coffee tree makes an attractive specimen tree for spacious landscapes. Ideal for parks and golf courses, it can also be included in large gardens.

Recommended

G. dioicus is a spreading tree with compound leaves up to 36" long, each consisting of many dark green to blue-green leaflets. It bears large clusters of white flowers in late spring or early summer. Leathery pods follow the flowers and ripen to reddish brown. The leaves turn yellow in fall. The ridged bark adds interest to the landscape in winter. Cultivars are available in compact forms and habits, with brilliant fall color and winter interest.

G. dioicus (above & below)

Don't panic if your Kentucky coffee tree hasn't started sprouting by May; it might not leaf out until mid-May.

This reliable tree rarely suffers from pest or disease problems.

Features: summer and fall foliage; fruit; bark; habit
Habit: upright to spreading, deciduous tree
Height: 50–75' **Spread:** 20–50' **Hardiness:** zones 3–8

Larch

Larix

L. laricina (above), L. decidua (below)

Larches are good trees for attracting birds to the garden.

The size of the low, weeping cultivars suits most residential gardens.

The larch makes an interesting specimen tree. It is one of the few needled trees that loses its foliage each year.

Growing
Larch grows best in **full sun**. The soil should be of **average fertility**, **acidic**, **moist** and **well drained**. Although tolerant of most conditions, this tree doesn't like dry or chalky soils.

Tips
This deciduous conifer likes cool, wet sites. It detests heat and drought, so careful placement is necessary.

Recommended
L. decidua (European larch) is a large, narrow, pyramidal tree with soft, green needles that turn bronzy yellow in fall. A weeping cultivar and a tall, conical variety exist as well. (Zones 3–6)

L. kaempferi (Japanese larch) is a tall specimen with pendulous branchlets. The summer color of the needles is bluer than that of European larch. Fall color is excellent. (Zones 4–7)

L. laricina (tamarack, Eastern larch) is an open, pyramidal tree with drooping branchlets. It grows very tall and narrow and is tolerant of wet locations. This native larch turns a rich, burnished gold in fall before losing its needles. (Zones 1–6)

Features: summer and fall foliage; habit
Habit: pyramidal, deciduous conifer
Height: 30–100' **Spread:** 12–40'
Hardiness: zones 1–7

Lilac
Syringa

There is no end to the colors, sizes, shapes and scents of lilacs available. An Iowa garden would be incomplete without at least one lilac.

Growing

Lilacs grow best in **full sun**. The soil should be **fertile, humus rich** and **well drained**. These plants tolerate open, windy locations.

Tips

Include lilacs in a shrub or mixed border, or use them to create an informal hedge. Japanese tree lilac can be used as a specimen tree.

Recommended

S. x chinensis (Chinese lilac) is a rounded shrub with arching branches and double, purple flowers. Cultivars and varieties are available. (Zones 4–8)

S. x hyacinthiflora (hyacinth-flowered lilac, early-flowering lilac) is a hardy, upright hybrid that becomes spreading as it matures. Clusters of fragrant flowers appear two weeks earlier than French lilacs. The leaves turn reddish purple in fall. (Zones 3–7)

S. meyeri (Meyer lilac) is a compact, rounded shrub that bears fragrant pink or lavender flowers. (Zones 3–7)

S. patula (Manchurian lilac) is an upright, vigorous shrub that offers cultivars in compact forms. (Zones 3–8)

S. x prestoniae (Preston lilac) is an extremely hardy, dense, mounding

S. *meyeri* TINKERBELLE (above), S. *vulgaris* (below)

shrub with crinkly foliage. It blooms approximately two weeks later than French lilacs.

S. vulgaris (French lilac, common lilac) is the shrub most people think of when they think of lilacs. It is a suckering, spreading shrub with an irregular habit that bears fragrant, lilac-colored flowers. (Zones 3–8)

Features: late-spring to mid-summer flowers; habit **Habit:** rounded, deciduous shrub or small tree **Flower color:** every shade of pink, purple and white **Height:** 4–25' **Spread:** 4–20' **Hardiness:** zones 2–8

Linden
Tilia

T. cordata (above)

Lindens are picturesque shade trees with a signature gumdrop shape and sweetly scented flowers that capture the essence of summer.

Growing
Lindens grow best in **full sun**. The soil should be **average to fertile, moist** and **well drained**. These trees adapt to most pH levels but prefer an alkaline soil. They tolerate urban conditions and pollution.

Tips
Lindens are useful and attractive street trees, shade trees and specimen trees. Their tolerance of pollution and their moderate size make lindens ideal for city gardens.

Recommended
T. americana (American linden, basswood) is a large tree with heart-shaped leaves and fragrant, yellow flowers. Cultivars are available.

T. cordata (littleleaf linden) is a dense, pyramidal tree that may become rounded with age. It bears small, fragrant flowers with narrow, yellow-green bracts. Cultivars are available.

T. mongolica (Mongolian linden) is an upright, round-headed tree with exfoliating bark and spectacular fall color. Cultivars are available.

T. tomentosa (silver linden) has a broad, pyramidal or rounded habit. It bears small, fragrant flowers and has glossy green leaves with fuzzy, silvery undersides.

Features: habit; foliage **Habit:** dense, pyramidal to rounded, deciduous tree **Height:** 30–45' **Spread:** 20–35' **Hardiness:** zones 3–8

Magnolia

Magnolia

Magnolias are beautiful, fragrant, versatile plants that also provide attractive winter structure.

Growing

Magnolias grow well in **full sun** or **partial shade**. The soil should be **fertile, humus rich, acidic, moist** and **well drained**. A summer mulch will help keep the roots cool and the soil moist.

Tips

Magnolias are used as specimen trees, and the smaller species can be used in borders.

Avoid planting magnolias where the morning sun will encourage the blooms to open too early in the season. Cold, wind and rain can damage the blossoms.

Recommended

Many species, hybrids and cultivars are available, in a range of sizes and with differing flowering times and flower colors. Three of the most common are *M. acuminata* (cucumber tree) is one of the most stately magnolias, growing into a wide, pyramidal shape. It bears dark green leaves with downy undersides and cup-shaped, lightly scented, greenish yellow flowers, followed by green, cucumber-shaped fruit that ripens to a deep red. *M.* x *soulangeana* (saucer magnolia) is a rounded, spreading, deciduous shrub or tree with pink,

M. stellata (above), *M.* x *soulangeana* (below)

purple or white flowers. *M. stellata* (star magnolia) is a compact, bushy or spreading, deciduous shrub or small tree, with fragrant, white flowers that have many petals. Check with your local nursery or garden center for other available magnolias.

Features: flowers; fruit; foliage; habit; bark
Habit: upright to spreading, deciduous shrub or tree **Flower color:** white, pink, purple, greenish yellow **Height:** 8–70' **Spread:** 5–30'
Hardiness: zones 4–8

Maple

Acer

A. *palmatum* var. *dissectum* (above)
A. *platanoides* 'Drummondii' (below)

Maples are attractive year-round, with attractive foliage and hanging samaras in summer, vibrant leaf color in fall, and interesting bark and branch structures in winter.

Growing

Generally, maples do well in **full sun** or **light shade,** though this varies from species to species. The soil should be **fertile, moist, high in organic matter** and **well drained.**

Tips

Maples can be used as specimen trees, as large elements in shrub or mixed borders or as hedges. Some are useful as understory plants bordering wooded areas; others can be grown in containers on patios or terraces. Most Japanese gardens showcase the attractive smaller maples. Almost all maples can be used to create bonsai specimens.

Recommended

Maples are some of the most popular trees used as shade or street trees. Many are very large when fully mature, but there are also a few smaller species that are useful in smaller gardens. A few of the more popular species are *A.* x *freemanii*, whose cultivars are far more popular. They grow quite tall and vary in habit and fall coloration. *A. palmatum* (Japanese maple) is a versatile tree species with many cultivars in smaller sizes that bear ornate, green and red foliage. *A. platanoides* (Norway maple) is a large, rounded tree with dense growth and good fall color. *A. rubrum* (red maple) is a tall, pyramidal tree when young but rounds out once mature, with varied fall color depending on the cultivar. *A. saccharum* (sugar maple) is considered to be the most impressive and majestic of all the maples. There are a vast array of species and cultivars to choose from. Consult your local garden center for additional discoveries.

Features: foliage; bark; winged fruit; fall color; form; small, inconspicuous flowers
Habit: deciduous; multi-stemmed tree or large shrub **Flower color:** yellowish green to a muted red **Height:** 15–80'
Spread: 15–70' **Hardiness:** zones 2–8

Northern Catalpa
Catalpa

Northern catalpa can reach grand heights in a relatively short span of time, resulting in a fine specimen for generations to come.

Growing

Northern catalpa prefers a **sunny** but sheltered position. The soil should be **moist** but **well drained**.

Tips

These trees can grow quite tall, producing a dense canopy of lush foliage but may look haggard when exposed to cold or dry winds or when planted in poor soil. Because of its size, this tree is best planted in a large, expansive but sheltered space as a specimen tree.

Recommended

C. speciosa (northern or western catalpa) is a vigorously growing, large tree with an open, narrow and irregular growth habit. This native tree is often grown for its large leaves and exotic, bell-shaped flowers. In mid-summer, the orchid-like flowers are borne in large, upright clusters, followed by bean-like seedpods or fruit. The long seedpods hang in clusters well into winter, offering an interesting winter display.

C. speciosa (above & below)

Northern catalpa is one of the most versatile and toughest trees available because of its adaptability to adverse conditions and locations.

Features: large leaves; flower clusters; decorative seedpods; hardiness; habit **Habit:** open, irregular canopy, narrow to oval crown **Flower color:** white, marked with purple and yellow **Height:** 40–60' **Spread:** 30–50' **Hardiness:** zones 4–8

Oak

Quercus

Q. *bicolor* (above)

The oak's classic shape, outstanding fall color, deep roots and long life are some of its many assets. Plant it for its individual beauty and for posterity.

Acorns are generally not edible. Those that are edible must usually be processed first to leach out the bitter tannins.

Growing

Oak grows well in **full sun** or **partial shade**. The soil should be **fertile, moist** and **well drained**. This tree can be difficult to establish; transplant it only when it is young.

Tips

Oak is a large tree that does best as a specimen or in a spacious yard, garden or public space. Do not disturb the ground around the base of an oak; this tree is very sensitive to changes in grade.

Recommended

The following are a few popular oak species. *Q. alba* (white oak) is a rounded, spreading tree with peeling bark; *Q. bicolor* (swamp white oak) is a broad, spreading tree that can tolerate wetter locations; *Q. imbricaria* (shingle oak, laurel oak) is a broad, spreading tree with smooth bark that has great fall color. *Q. macrocarpa* (bur or mossycup oak) is a stately, medium-sized tree with an open and upright habit, an oval crown, very large and deeply lobed leaves, and bark that is deeply textured and looks corky. *Q. muehlenbergii* (chinkapin oak, yellow chestnut oak) is an open, rounded tree with scaly bark and good fall color. *Q. rubra* (red oak) is a rounded, spreading tree with fall color ranging from yellow to red-brown. Many cultivars are available for each species; check with your local nursery or garden center.

Features: summer and fall foliage; bark; habit; acorns **Habit:** large, rounded, spreading, deciduous tree **Height:** 40–100' **Spread:** 40–100' **Hardiness:** zones 3–8

Ornamental Pear

Pyrus

Ornamental pear trees flower reliably with a dazzling display of white in spring, followed by good green foliage and relatively strong fall color.

Growing

Ornamental pear trees grow best in **full sun.** The soil should be **fertile** and **well drained,** but these trees adapt to most soil conditions and tolerate drought and pollution.

Very little pruning is needed; remove awkward, crossed and damaged branches in early spring.

Tips

Ornamental pear trees make excellent specimen trees. They can be quite messy when the fruit ripens, so plant them away from parked cars, patios and decks, and be prepared for some cleanup around the tree. The fruit of ornamental pears and their cultivars are not considered edible.

Ornamental pear trees, like apple trees, can be trained to form espalier specimens against a wall or fence.

Recommended

P. calleryana (Callery pear) is a thorny, irregular, conical tree rarely grown in favor of the cultivars. 'Aristocrat' is a fast-growing, broadly pyramidal, thornless tree. It has shiny, dark green foliage that is tinged purple when young, becoming a brilliant deep red in fall. The flowers are white, and the fruit is red to yellow. 'Autumn Blaze' has an

P. calleryana CHANTICLEER (above), *P. calleryana* (below)

irregular, open crown and horizontal branching. It is known for its bright red to purple fall color. CHANTICLEER ('Glen's Form,' 'Select,' 'Cleveland Select,' 'Stone Hill') has a narrow, pyramidal form. It blooms profusely in spring, and its leaves turn red in fall. It is fairly resistant to fire blight. Many other cultivars are also available, but they are beginning to show susceptibility to fire blight.

Features: early- to mid-spring flowers; fruit; habit; bark; fall foliage **Habit:** columnar to broadly pyramidal, deciduous tree
Flower color: white **Height:** 35–50'
Spread: 15–30' **Hardiness:** zones 5–8

Pine

Pinus

P. ponderosa (above), P. strobus (below)

Pines offer exciting possibilities for any garden. Exotic-looking pines are available with soft or stiff, silvery blue or gray needles; elegant, drooping branches; and flaky, copper-colored bark.

Growing

Pines grow best in **full sun**. These trees adapt to most **well-drained** soils but do not tolerate polluted urban conditions.

Tips

Pines can be used as specimen trees, hedges or windbreaks. Smaller cultivars can be included in shrub or mixed borders. These trees are not heavy feeders; fertilizing will encourage rapid new growth that is weak and susceptible to pest and disease problems.

Recommended

The number of pines to choose from, including both trees and shrubby dwarf plants, is vast. Check with your local garden center or nursery to find out what is available for your yard or garden.

Pine varieties generally thrive in our Iowa climate; however, some pine species and cultivars are susceptible to both windburn and sunscald. Consult your local garden center for their recommendations.

Features: foliage; bark; cones; habit
Habit: upright, columnar or spreading, evergreen tree **Height:** 3–65' **Spread:** 3–25'
Hardiness: zones 2–8

Potentilla

Potentilla (Pentaphylloides)

Potentilla is a fuss-free shrub that blooms madly throughout summer.

Growing

Potentilla prefers **full sun** but tolerates partial or light shade. Preferably, the soil should be of **poor to average fertility** and **well drained**. This plant tolerates most conditions, including sandy or clay soil and wet or dry conditions. Established plants are drought tolerant. Too much fertilizer or too rich a soil will encourage weak, floppy, disease-prone growth.

Tips

Potentilla is useful in a shrub or mixed border. The smaller cultivars can be included in rock gardens and on rock walls. On steep slopes, potentilla can prevent soil erosion and reduce time spent maintaining the lawn. It can even be used to form a low, informal hedge.

If your potentilla's flowers fade in direct sun or hot weather, move the plant to a cooler location that provides shade from the hot afternoon sun. Colors should revive in fall when the weather cools. Yellow-flowered plants are least likely to be affected by heat and sun.

P. fruticosa (above & below)

Recommended

Of the many cultivars of *P. fruticosa* (*Pentaphylloides floribunda*), the following are a few of the most popular and interesting. '**Abbotswood**' is one of the best white-flowered cultivars, '**Pink Beauty**' bears pink, semi-double flowers, '**Tangerine**' has orange flowers and '**Yellow Gem**' has bright yellow flowers.

Also called: shrubby cinquefoil, golden hardhack
Features: flowers; foliage; habit **Habit:** mounding, deciduous shrub **Flower color:** yellow, white, pink, orange **Height:** 3"–4' **Spread:** 12–36"
Hardiness: zones 2–8

Redbud

Cercis

C. *canadensis* (above & below)

Redbud is not as long-lived as many other trees, so use its delicate beauty to supplement more permanent trees in the garden.

Redbud is an outstanding treasure of spring. Deep magenta flowers bloom before the leaves emerge, and their impact is intense. As the buds open, the flowers turn pink, covering the long, thin branches in pastel clouds.

Growing

Redbud grows well in **full sun, partial shade** or **light shade**. The soil should be a **fertile, deep loam** that is **moist** and **well drained**. This plant has tender roots and does not like being transplanted.

Tips

Redbud can be used as a specimen tree in a shrub or mixed border or in a woodland garden.

Recommended

C. canadensis (eastern redbud) is a spreading, multistemmed tree that bears red, purple or pink flowers. The young foliage is bronze, fading to green over summer and turning bright yellow in fall. Many beautiful cultivars are available.

Features: spring flowers; fall foliage
Habit: rounded or spreading, multistemmed, deciduous tree or shrub
Flower color: magenta, red, purple, pink **Height:** 20–30' **Spread:** 25–35'
Hardiness: zones 4–8

Rhododendron/Azalea

Rhododendron

Even without their flowers, rhododendrons are wonderful landscape plants. Their striking, dark green foliage lends an interesting texture to a shrub planting in summer.

Growing

Rhododendrons prefer **partial shade** or **light shade,** but they tolerate full sun in a site with adequate moisture. A location sheltered from strong winds is preferable. The soil should be **fertile, humus rich, acidic, moist** and very **well drained.** Rhododendrons are sensitive to high pH, salinity and winter injury.

Tips

Use rhododendrons and azaleas in shrub or mixed borders, in woodland gardens, as specimen plants, in group plantings, as hedges and informal barriers, in rock gardens or in planters on a shady patio or balcony.

Rhododendrons and azaleas are generally grouped together. Extensive breeding and hybridizing is making it more and more difficult to label them separately.

Recommended

In our area, we can grow many different rhododendron and azalea species and cultivars. Many wonderful nurseries and specialty growers can help you find the right rhododendron or azalea for your garden.

Features: late-winter to early-summer flowers; foliage; habit **Habit:** upright, mounding, rounded, evergreen or deciduous shrub **Flower color:** white, pink, purple, cream, salmon, red, bicolored **Height:** 2–12' **Spread:** 2–12' **Hardiness:** zones 3–8

Serviceberry
Amelanchier

A. canadensis (above), *A. laevis* (below)

The *Amelanchier* species are first-rate North American natives, bearing lacy, white flowers in spring followed by edible berries. In fall, the foliage color ranges from a glowing apricot to deep red.

Serviceberry fruit can be used in place of blueberries in any recipe because they have a similar, but generally sweeter, flavor.

Growing

Serviceberries grow well in **full sun** or **light shade**. They prefer **acidic** soil that is **fertile, humus rich, moist** and **well drained**. They do adjust to drought.

Tips

With their often artistic branch growth, serviceberries make beautiful specimen plants, or even as shade trees in small gardens. The shrubbier forms can be grown along the edges of a woodland or in a border. In the wild, these trees are often found growing near water sources; they are beautiful beside ponds or streams.

Recommended

Several species and hybrids are available. A few popular serviceberries are *A. alnifolia* (serviceberry, Saskatoon, Juneberry), a native shrub with white flowers and edible, blue-black fruit; *A. canadensis* (shadblow serviceberry), a large, upright, suckering shrub with white flowers, purple fruit and good fall color; and *A. x grandiflora* (apple serviceberry), a small, spreading, often multi-stemmed tree. The new foliage is a bronze color, turning green in summer and bright orange or red in fall. White, spring flowers are followed by edible, purple fruit in summer. *A. laevis* (Allegheny serviceberry) is a tree with a spreading habit. The new leaves are reddish, turning green in summer and scarlet in fall. White, mid-spring flowers are followed by sweet, dark blue fruit.

Also called: Saskatoon, Juneberry **Features:** spring or early-summer flowers; edible fruit; fall color; habit; bark **Habit:** single- or multi-stemmed, deciduous, large shrub or small tree **Flower color:** white **Height:** 15–25' **Spread:** 15–20' **Hardiness:** zones 3–8

Spirea
Spiraea

S. japonica 'Goldmound' (above), *S. x vanhouttei* (below)

Spirea, seen in so many gardens and with dozens of cultivars, remains an undeniable favorite. With a wide range of forms, sizes and colors of both foliage and flowers, spirea has many possible uses in the landscape.

Growing

Spirea prefers **full sun**. To help prevent foliage burn, provide protection from very hot sun. The soil should be **fertile, acidic, moist** and **well drained**.

Tips

Spirea is used in shrub or mixed borders, in rock gardens and as informal screens and hedges.

Recommended

The following are a few of the most popular hybrid groups of the many species and cultivars available. *S. x bumalda* (*S. japonica* 'Bumalda') is a low, broad, mounded shrub with pink flowers. It is rarely grown in favor of the many cultivars, which also have pink flowers, but with brightly colored foliage. *S. japonica* (Japanese spirea) forms a clump of erect stems and bears pink or white flowers. *S. nipponica* (Nippon spirea) forms an upright shrub with arching branches. White flowers appear in mid-summer. *S. x vanhouttei* (bridal wreath spirea, Vanhoutte spirea) is a dense, bushy shrub with arching branches that bears clusters of white flowers. Check your local nursery or garden center for additional varieties and cultivars.

Features: summer flowers; habit
Habit: round, bushy, deciduous shrub
Flower color: pink, white **Height:** 3–8'
Spread: 3–8' **Hardiness:** zones 3–8

Spruce
Picea

P. glauca 'Conica' (above)
P. pungens var. glauca 'Moerheim' (below)

Spruce tree and shrub specimens are some of the most commonly grown evergreens in Iowa. Grow spruces where they have enough room to spread; then, let them branch all the way to the ground.

Growing
Spruce trees grow best in **full sun**. The soil should be **deep, moist, well drained** and **neutral to acidic**. These trees generally don't like hot, dry or polluted conditions. They are best grown from small, young stock because they dislike being transplanted when they are larger or more mature.

Tips
Spruces are used as specimen trees. The dwarf and slow-growing cultivars can also be used in shrub or mixed borders. These trees look most attractive when allowed to keep their lower branches.

Recommended
Spruces are generally upright pyramidal trees, but cultivars may be low-growing, wide-spreading or even weeping in habit. *P. abies* (Norway spruce), *P. glauca* (white spruce), *P. pungens* (Colorado spruce) and their cultivars are popular and commonly available.

Oil-based pesticides such as dormant oil can take the blue out of your blue-needled spruce.

Features: foliage; cones; habit **Habit:** conical or columnar, evergreen tree or shrub **Height:** 2–65'
Spread: 2–30' **Hardiness:** zones 2–8

Sumac

Rhus

Sumacs are unique foliar specimens, ideally suited to contemporary designs where they can exhibit their colorful attributes and architectural form.

Growing
Sumacs develop the best fall color in **full sun,** but they tolerate partial shade. They prefer soil that is of **average fertility, moist** and **well drained**. Once established, sumacs tolerate drought very well.

Tips
Sumacs can be used to form a specimen group in a shrub or mixed border, on a sloping bank or in a woodland garden. Both male and female plants are needed for fruit to form.

Recommended
R. aromatica (fragrant sumac) forms a low mound of suckering stems and has clusters of small, yellow flowers that appear in spring. Fuzzy fruit that turns red as it ripens follows the flowers in late spring. The aromatic foliage turns red or purple in fall. Many cultivars are available.

R. coppalina (flameleaf sumac, shining sumac, dwarf sumac) is a dense, compact grower when young, becoming more open and irregular as it matures. It grows quite tall, bearing clusters of creamy flowers in mid- to late summer, followed by fuzzy, red fruit in fall. Both the species and cultivars offer great fall color.

R. glabra (smooth sumac) is an upright, spreading shrub that grows in colonies as it suckers. The green foliage turns orange, red and purple in fall. Scarlet

R. *typhina* (above), R. *aromatica* (below)

fruit follows the flowers. Various cultivars are available. (Zones 2–8)

R. trilobata (skunkbush sumac) is a slow-growing, upright shrub of medium size. The leaves are fragrant when crushed and turn a brilliant auburn red in fall. Cultivars are available in a spreading form.

R. typhina (*R. hirta;* staghorn sumac) is a suckering, colony-forming shrub with branches covered in velvety fuzz. Fuzzy, yellow, early-summer flowers are followed by hairy, red fruit. The leaves turn stunning shades of yellow, orange and red in fall.

Features: summer and fall foliage; fall fruit
Habit: deciduous, low-growing or upright shrub
Flower color: greenish yellow **Height:** 2½–30'
Spread: 5–30' **Hardiness:** zones 3–8

Viburnum

Viburnum

V. plicatum 'Mariesii' (above)
V. lantana 'Mohican' (below)

Good fall color, attractive form, shade tolerance, scented flowers and attractive fruit puts viburnum in a class by itself.

Growing

Viburnum grows well in **full sun, partial shade or light shade**. The soil should be of **average fertility, moist** and **well drained**. Viburnum tolerates both alkaline and acidic soils.

Most berries are inedible or eaten only by birds as winter forage. Only a few species produce edible berries.

Tips

Viburnum can be used in borders and woodland gardens. It is a good choice for planting near decks and patios.

Recommended

Many viburnum species, hybrids and cultivars are available. *V. x carlesii* (Korean spice viburnum) is a dense, bushy, rounded shrub that bears white or pink, spicy-scented flowers, followed by red fruit ripening to black.
V. dentatum (arrowwood) is a large shrub with coarse leaves and white flowers followed by rounded, bluish black fruit. *V. x juddii* (Judd viburnum) is a rounded shrub with fragrant, white flowers followed by red fruit that turns black. It has great fall color. *V. lantana* (wayfaring tree) is a stout, globe-shaped shrub with leathery, gray-green foliage that turns purplish red in fall. Clusters of creamy white flowers emerge in spring followed by reddish black berries. *V. lentago* (nannyberry) is a large, upright shrub and produces shiny green foliage that turns a deep purple-red in fall. Flat-topped clusters of creamy white flowers emerge in spring, followed by bluish black berries. *V. plicatum* (Japanese snowball viburnum) is a bushy, upright shrub with horizontal branching. Ball-like clusters of white flowers appear in late spring. Fall color is reddish purple. Cultivars are available for each species in varied forms, sizes and overall appeal.

Features: flowers (some fragrant); summer and fall foliage; fruit; habit **Habit:** bushy or spreading, evergreen, semi-evergreen or deciduous shrub **Flower color:** white, pink **Height:** 2–20' **Spread:** 2–10' **Hardiness:** zones 2–8

Witch-Hazel

Hamamelis

itch-hazel is an investment in happiness. It blooms in early spring, the flowers last for weeks, and their spicy fragrance awakens the senses. Then in fall, the handsome leaves develop overlapping bands of orange, yellow and red.

Growing

Witch-hazel grows best in a sheltered spot with **full sun** or **light shade.** The soil should be of **average fertility, neutral to acidic, moist** and **well drained.**

Tips

Witch-hazel works well individually or in groups. It can be used as a specimen plant, in shrub or mixed borders or in woodland gardens. As small trees, they are ideal for space-limited gardens.

The unique flowers have long, narrow, crinkled petals that give the plant a spidery appearance when in bloom. If the weather gets too cold, the petals will roll up, protecting the flowers and extending the flowering season.

Recommended

H. x *intermedia* is a vase-shaped, spreading shrub that bears fragrant clusters of yellow, orange or red flowers. The leaves turn attractive shades of orange, red and bronze in fall. Cultivars with flowers in shades of red, yellow or orange are available, including 'Arnold Promise,' 'Diane,' 'Jelena' and '**Primavera.**' (Zones 5–9)

H. vernalis (above)

H. vernalis (vernal witchhazel, Ozark witch-hazel) is a rounded, upright, often suckering shrub. Very fragrant, yellow, orange or red flowers are borne in early spring. The foliage turns bright yellow in fall.

The branches of spring-blooming witch-hazels can be cut in winter and forced into bloom indoors.

Features: fragrant, early-spring flowers; summer and fall foliage; habit **Habit:** spreading, deciduous shrub or small tree **Flower color:** yellow, orange, red **Height:** 6–20' **Spread:** 6–20' **Hardiness:** zones 4–8

Yew

Taxus

T. x media 'Fairview' (above), *T. cuspidata* (below)

Growing

Yews grow well in any light condition from **full sun to full shade**. The soil should be **fertile, moist** and **well drained**. These trees tolerate windy, dry and polluted conditions and soils of any acidity, but they cannot tolerate excessive soil moisture. They also dislike excessive heat and, if they are on the hotter south or southwest side of a building, may suffer needle scorch.

Tips

Yews can be used in borders or as specimens, hedges, topiaries and groundcovers.

Male and female flowers are borne on separate plants. Both must be present for the attractive red seed cups to form.

Recommended

T. cuspidata (Japanese yew) is an upright but irregularly V-shaped shrub with sharply pointed, needle-like leaves. A pyramidal cultivar is available.

T. x media (Anglojap yew), a cross between *T. baccata* (English yew) and *T. cuspidata* (Japanese yew), has the vigor of the English yew and the cold hardiness of the Japanese yew. It forms a rounded, upright tree or shrub, though the size and form can vary among the many cultivars. A few attractive selections include 'Brownii,' 'Capitata,' 'Densiformis,' 'Everlow' and 'Hicksii.'

From sweeping hedges to commanding specimens, yews can serve many purposes in the garden. They are some of the most reliable evergreens for deep shade.

All parts of yews are poisonous, except for the pleasant-tasting, fleshy, red cup that surrounds the inedible hard seed.

Features: foliage; habit; red seed cups **Habit:** evergreen; conical or columnar tree; bushy or spreading shrub **Height:** 2–50' **Spread:** 4–30' **Hardiness:** zones 4–7

Bonica
Floribunda

Bonica was the first modern shrub rose to be named an All-America Selection. The blooms have a light, sweet fragrance, and bright orange hips follow the double, pink flowers.

Growing

Bonica prefers **full sun** and **fertile, moist, well-drained** soil with at least **5% organic matter** mixed in. It can tolerate light breezes, but keep it out of strong winds. Roses are heavy feeders and drinkers, and they do not like to share their root space with other plants. This disease-resistant, hardy rose tolerates shade and poor soils.

Tips

Bonica suits just about any location. Rose growers recommend it for mixed beds, containers, hedges, cut-flower gardens or as a groundcover, standard or specimen.

Recommended

Rosa 'Bonica' is a tidy, spreading rose of modest size that blooms profusely throughout most of the growing season. It bears an abundance of semi-glossy, rich green foliage that is beautiful enough to stand on its own.

This beautiful rose has maintained worldwide popularity since its introduction.

Also called: Bonica '82, Meidomonac, Demon, Bonica Meidiland
Features: repeat blooming; summer to fall flowers; easy maintenance; colorful hips
Flower color: medium pink **Height:** 3–5'
Spread: 3–4' **Hardiness:** zones 4–9

Carefree Beauty

Modern Shrub Rose

This magnificent rose was developed by the late Dr. Griffith J. Buck at Iowa State University. It is one in the long line of Dr. Buck's 'prairie' show-stoppers that are perfectly suited to Iowa gardens.

Growing

Carefree Beauty requires a location in **full sun**. Well-drained, **organically rich**, **slightly acidic** soil is best, but this shrub rose tolerates slight shade and poorer soils.

Tips

This upright shrub has a spreading habit, which makes it an ideal candidate for a low-maintenance hedge. It also makes a fine specimen and will complement other flowering shrubs and perennials in mixed borders.

Recommended

Rosa 'Carefree Beauty' bears small clusters of deep pink, 4½" wide, semi-double blossoms, not once but twice, throughout the growing season. The blossoms are large, which balances out the small quantities of flowers produced at the end of each stem. The fragrant flowers beautifully complement the smooth, olive-green foliage. Orange-red hips follow after the flowers, adding winter interest to the landscape into the early months of spring.

Carefree Beauty was introduced into the marketplace in 1977. It was the result of crossing an unidentified rose seedling with 'Prairie Princess.'

Also called: Audace **Features:** fragrant, large blossoms; disease-free foliage; vigorous growth habit **Flower color:** deep pink
Height: 5–6' **Spread:** 4–5'
Hardiness: zones 3–9

Carefree Delight
Modern Shrub

The name of this shrub rose is perfectly appropriate. Part of a series of Meidiland landscape roses, Carefree Delight is just that—carefree.

Growing
This repeat-blooming rose prefers **full to partial sun**. The soil should be of **average fertility** and **well drained**. It doesn't require much deadheading. It produces vast quantities of showy rose hips in fall and, like all roses with a low petal count, it tolerates some shade.

Tips
Carefree Delight is used most often along borders but is also useful for hedging and mass planting. It is consistent in all climates, making it suitable for just about any setting or region. It is almost evergreen in areas with warmer winter temperatures, and in areas with colder winters, the foliage changes to bronzy red in fall.

Recommended
Rosa 'Carefree Delight' requires little care and produces a delightful display of single, carmine-pink blossoms amid dark, glossy foliage. It is an ideal landscape rose and is almost always in bloom. The flowers emerge in large clusters and continue to bloom in waves throughout summer.

Carefree Delight won the AARS designation in 1996, one of only a few shrub roses to receive this honor.

Also called: Bingo Meidiland, Bingo Meillandecor, Evermore **Features:** 1½–2½" wide, single blossoms; repeat blooming **Flower color:** carmine pink with a white eye **Height:** 3½–4' **Spread:** 3½–4' **Hardiness:** zones 4–9

Dart's Dash
Rugosa Rose

Like other hybrid rugosa roses, Dart's Dash is easy to grow, resistant to diseases and will thrive in the poorest of conditions.

Growing
Dart's Dash prefers **full to partial sun**. The soil should be **well drained** and **slightly acidic** with added **organic material**.

This easy-to-grow rugosa is ideal for cutting and for fresh arrangements. Plentiful rose hips will provide winter interest well into spring.

Tips
This rugosa is often used along borders or for short hedging. It is also considered to be a groundcover rose by some because of its vigorous and dense growth habit.

Recommended
Rosa 'Dart's Dash' is a small sport of *Rosa rugosa*. The single, dark red flowers emerge in repeated blooming cycles, first in late spring and again later in summer, resulting in blossoms almost all season long. This rose serves up an attractive supply of hips in fall.

Features: fragrant, single flowers; disease resistance; vigorous growth habit **Flower color:** deep red with yellow centers **Height:** 3–4' **Spread:** 3–4' **Hardiness:** zones 3–10

Flower Carpet

Modern Shrub Rose

Since their release in 1991, Flower Carpet roses have proven themselves to be low-maintenance, blackspot-resistant, long-blooming performers in the landscape.

Growing
Flower Carpet roses grow best in **full sun**. The soil should be **average to fertile, humus rich, slightly acidic, moist** and **well drained,** but these hardy roses are fairly adaptable.

Tips
Although not true groundcovers, these small shrub roses have a dense and spreading habit useful for filling in large areas. They can also be used as low hedges or in mixed borders, but the occasional long, rangy cane may require some pruning to reduce the spread. Flower Carpet roses even grow well near roads, sidewalks and driveways where salt is applied in winter.

Recommended
The *Rosa* 'Flower Carpet' series of roses are bushy, low-growing, spreading plants with shiny, bright green, leathery foliage. They produce single or semi-double flowers in white, pink, coral, red, pale yellow or appleblossom, with prominent yellow stamens. These flowers last from early summer through fall to the first heavy frost.

These roses bloom in such abundance that the flowers form a carpet, hence the name Flower Carpet. Deadheading will keep the plants tidy and blooming enthusiastically.

Features: mounding, spreading habit; summer through fall flowers **Flower color:** deep, hot pink, white, coral, red, appleblossom **Height:** 30–36"
Spread: 3–4' **Hardiness:** zones 4–8

Graham Thomas

English or Austin Rose

Cnglish roses such as Graham Thomas are unique and well suited to the Iowa landscape. Their delicate exterior often disguises a tough disposition and willingness to thrive.

Graham Thomas was developed in 1983 by David Austin Roses Ltd., and was the first true yellow English rose. It was named after one of the most influential rosarians of our time. Graham Thomas received the Royal Horticultural Society Award of Garden Merit in 1993.

Growing

Graham Thomas prefers **full sun** but tolerates slight shade. The soil should be **well drained**, **organically rich** and **moist**. Deadheading may be required to extend the prolific blooming cycle. Wet weather will not trouble this rose, but do not plant it in areas that may be too hot because the heat causes reduced flowering and fades the flower color.

Tips

In warmer climates, this extremely vigorous rose will grow to a greater height if it is supported, developing into a pillar style or climbing rose. A light pruning will allow Graham Thomas to remain a little smaller if desired, but this may naturally occur in cooler climates.

Recommended

Rosa 'Graham Thomas' bears beautiful, apricot pink buds that open into large, golden yellow blooms. The double blooms carry up to 35 petals and fade gracefully with time. The flowers remain cupped until the petals fall cleanly from the plant. This rose is very dense and upright in form, bearing an abundance of light green leaves. It is a repeat bloomer, beginning its first prolific cycle in early summer. There are many English roses to choose from, ranging in color from pink, antique white, apricot or yellow. Consult your local garden center for recommendations.

Also called: English Yellow, Graham Stuart Thomas
Features: strongly scented, 4–5" wide flowers; color; form
Flower color: pink, yellow, white, apricot **Height:** 3½–7'
Spread: 4–5' **Hardiness:** zones 5b–9

Knockout
Modern Shrub Rose

$\mathcal{T}$his rose is simply one of the best new shrub roses to hit the market in years. It is considered to be virtually indestructible and was sure to become a favorite—and did it ever!

Growing
Knockout prefers **full sun**. The hotter the weather, the better this rose performs. The flower color tends to display more red in cooler weather, however. The soil should be **well drained** and of **average fertility**.

Tips
Knockout is just what its name suggests when planted en masse or as a specimen. Its rounded, well-behaved form is ideal for just about any garden setting. This rose responds best to light deadheading and pruning.

Recommended
Rosa 'Knockout' bears single flowers made up of 5–11 petals in small clusters atop truly disease-resistant foliage. The moderately scented flowers average 3–3½" in width, first emerging in summer only to bloom once again well into fall. Fall color is another showy feature of this rose; the semi-glossy, dark green leaves transform into shades of burgundy as the days grow colder. Orange-red hips emerge once the flowers are spent and last well into winter.

An AARS winner in 2000, this rose is totally carefree and rarely without flowers.

Conard-Pyle sold over 700,000 Knockout roses in only two years, a great accomplishment for William Radler, the originator of this rose.

Features: fragrant blossoms; color; form; disease resistance; prolific blooming
Flower color: deep but bright red pink
Height: 3' **Spread:** 3' **Hardiness:** zones 4–10

Magnifica
Rugosa Rose

Rugosa roses are a tried and true group of reliable and hardy specimens that will thrive even in the most adverse conditions.

Growing
Magnifica requires **full sun to partial shade** in order to thrive. **Well-drained, moist** soil of **average fertility** is best.

Magnifica was developed by Dr. Walter Van Fleet in the U.S. and released in 1905. He was also the breeder of New Dawn, a true classic.

Tips
This hardy rugosa rose is ideal for use as a groundcover. Its dense growth habit, lush foliage and prolific flowering cycles will cover an unsightly embankment or slope in a year or two. It also works well in mixed borders and small groupings for impact.

Recommended
Rosa 'Magnifica' produces double, cupped-shaped blooms. The fragrant blooms are borne in shades of reddish purple with white centers and prominent yellow stamens. The foliage is lush and scented as well.

Also called: Rugosa Magnifica, Rosa 'Rugosa Magnifica'
Features: intensely scented flowers; flower color; low growth habit **Flower color:** reddish purple **Height:** 24–36"
Spread: 4–5' **Hardiness:** zones 4–10

Nearly Wild

Floribunda Rose

Nearly Wild is one of the hardiest floribunda roses and one of the first to bloom in spring.

Growing

Nearly Wild prefers **full sun** but tolerates partial shade. The soil should be of **average to poor fertility**, **moist**, **well drained** and **slightly acidic**.

Tips

Although it looks wild, Nearly Wild's growth habit is quite tame. The plant is nicely rounded and dense, making it ideal as a short hedge.

Recommended

Rosa 'Nearly Wild' bears small, long, pointed buds that open into single, medium pink blossoms with a central, white eye. The moderately sweet, apple-scented blossoms are made up of five petals each, resulting in a simple yet classic form. The flowers are borne in clusters on long, straight stems atop a bushy form. Nearly Wild blooms prolifically, and the flowers almost totally obscure the foliage underneath.

This rose was hybridized by H.C. Brownell in 1941. If introduced today, this tough little rose would probably be sold as a shrub rose.

Features: 2–2½" wide flowers; repeat blooming habit; hardiness
Flower color: medium pink with a white center **Height:** 24–36" **Spread:** 24–36"
Hardiness: zones 4–10

Ramblin' Red

Climbing Rose

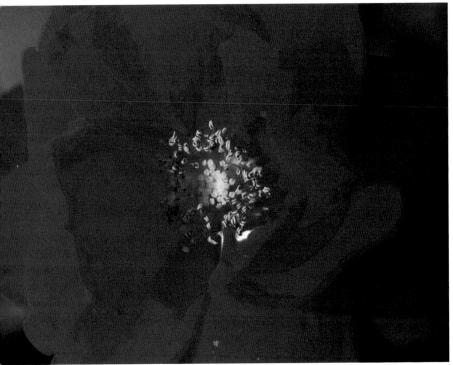

Not only is this climbing rose hardy, but it's also beautiful, boasting 5" wide, deep red blossoms on long, sturdy stems that are covered in lush, disease-resistant foliage.

Growing

Ramblin' Red prefers a location in **full sun**. The soil should be **moist**, of **average fertility** and **well drained**.

The flowers are long lasting, whether on the plant or in a vase.

Ramblin' Red was the result of crossing the floribunda Razzle Dazzle and winter-hardy climber Henry Kelsey. It was bred by William J. Radler of the U.S. and introduced by Bailey Nursery in 2002.

Tips

This rose features exquisitely formed, nonfading, double blooms. With its long, vigorous shoots, Ramblin' Red is ideal for training to climb pillars, pergolas, trellises and arbors.

Recommended

Rosa 'Ramblin' Red' bears fully double blooms borne in clusters. Each blossom is made up of 26–40 petals. This winter-hardy climber has strong, pliable canes clothed in disease-resistant foliage. The newest foliage is infused with red and turns a deep green.

Features: repeat blooming habit; slightly fragrant, double blooms **Flower color:** medium red **Height:** 8–10' **Spread:** variable, dependent on support **Hardiness:** zones 3–9

The Fairy
Modern Shrub Rose

The Fairy is popular with novice and experienced gardeners. It bears large clusters of dainty, soft pink, rosette-shaped, double flowers.

Growing
The Fairy grows well in **full sun or partial shade**, in **fertile, moist, well-drained** soil with at least 5% **organic matter** mixed in. It is prone to blackspot when planted in partial shade, but will still bloom. Roses can tolerate light breezes, but keep them out of strong winds. These heavy feeders and drinkers do not like to share their root space with other plants. The Fairy's flower color fades more slowly in partial shade.

Tips
This rose can be used in containers, as groundcovers, in mixed beds and borders, as a weeping standard, or left to trail over a low wall or embankment. It looks great massed or planted as low hedging. It also makes a beautiful cut flower.

Recommended
Rosa 'The Fairy' is a compact mounding plant with moderately prickly canes and glossy foliage. It is trouble free and moderately resistant to disease. It blooms continually until fall frost.

This rose doesn't just tolerate neglect, it prefers it. It manages successfully in partial shade, and the shade slows the fading of the flower color.

Features: repeat blooming, late summer to fall flowers; low maintenance **Flower color:** soft pink **Height:** 24" **Spread:** 2–4' **Hardiness:** zones 4–9

William Baffin

Shrub, Explorer Rose

Tough and versatile, hardy and vigorous, this rose meets all expectations. William Baffin is highly disease resistant and requires very little to no maintenance. It is thought to be the best shrub or climbing rose for colder regions.

Growing
William Baffin prefers **full sun** but tolerates afternoon shade. **Average to fertile**, **slightly acidic** soil that's **rich with organic matter** works best. The soil should also be **moist** and **well drained**.

Tips
William Baffin is tall enough to be trained as a climber or pillar rose. It is hardy enough to remain on a trellis, arbor or pergola in the coldest of winters, requiring no pruning or any special winter protection.

Recommended
Rosa **'William Baffin'** bears semi-double flowers borne in clusters of 30 or more. Glossy, medium-green foliage is vigorously produced in dense mounds on wiry, stiff stems.

This rose was named after the famous explorer who discovered Lancaster Sound while he searched for the Northwest Passage in 1616.

Features: vigorous, hardy climber; lightly scented, summer flowers that repeat in fall
Flower color: deep pink **Height:** 8–10'
Spread: 5–6' **Hardiness:** zones 2–8

Akebia
Akebia

A. quinata (above & below)

This vigorous vine will twine up anything that gets in its way. It can become invasive, so keep the pruning shears handy if you plan to sit near it.

Growing

Akebia grows equally well in **full sun**, **light shade** or **partial shade** in **well-drained** soil of **average to high fertility**. It tolerates dry or moist soils and full shade.

Tips

Although the flowers and fruit are interesting, this vine is worth growing for its foliage alone. Akebia will quickly cover any sturdy structure, such as a porch railing, trellis, pergola, arbor or fence. Cut back the plant as much and as often as needed to keep it under control.

Recommended

A. x *pentaphylla* is a semi-evergreen, climbing vine with rounded leaves, divided into three to five or more leaflets that take on a purple tinge in winter. Fragrant, purple, cup-shaped flowers emerge in early spring, followed by dangling fruit clusters.

A. quinata (fiveleaf akebia, chocolate vine) is a fast-growing, twining, deciduous climbing vine. The new foliage is tinged purple in spring and matures to an attractive blue green. Deep purple flowers are borne in spring followed by sausage-like fruit pods. '**Alba**' bears white flowers and fruit.

A. trifoliata (three-leaf akebia) is a deciduous climber with rounded leaves that are divided into three or more leaflets, opening bronze and then becoming a glossy, dark green with maturity. Purple flowers are produced in spring and followed by fruit.

Also called: fiveleaf akebia **Features:** foliage; habit; flowers; fruit **Flower color:** purple, white
Height: 20–40' **Spread:** 20–40' **Hardiness:** zones 4–8

Boston Ivy

Parthenocissus

P. tricuspidata (above), P. quinquefolia (below)

Virginia creeper can cover the sides of buildings and help keep them cool in summer heat. Cut the plants back to keep windows and doors accessible.

Boston ivy is a handsome vine that establishes quickly and provides an air of age and permanence, even on new structures.

Growing
This vine grows well in any light from **full sun to full shade**. The soil should be **fertile** and **well drained**. Boston ivy will adapt to clay or sandy soils.

Tips
Boston ivy has clinging rootlets that can adhere to just about any surface, even smooth wood, vinyl or metal. Give this plant a lot of space and let it cover walls, fences or arbors.

Recommended
The following two species are very similar, except for the shape of the leaves.

P. quinquefolia (Virginia creeper, woodbine) has dark green foliage. Each leaf, divided into five leaflets, turns flame red in fall.

P. tricuspidata (Boston ivy, Japanese creeper) has dark green, three-lobed leaves that turn red in fall. This species is not quite as hardy as Virginia creeper.

Features: summer and fall foliage; clinging habit
Height: 30–70' **Spread:** 30–70'
Hardiness: zones 3–8

Clematis

Clematis

C. x *jackmanii* cultivar (above & below)

There are so many species, hybrids and cultivars of clematis that it is possible to have one in bloom all season.

Growing

Clematis prefers **full sun** but tolerates partial shade. The soil should be **fertile, humus rich, moist** and **well drained**. This vine enjoys warm, sunny weather, but the roots prefer to be cool. A thick layer of mulch or a planting of low, shade-providing perennials will protect the tender roots. Clematis is quite cold hardy but will fare best when protected from winter wind. The rootball of vining clematis should be planted about 2" beneath the surface of the soil.

Tips

Clematis can climb up structures, such as trellises, railings, fences or arbors. It can also be allowed to grow over shrubs or up trees and can be used as groundcover.

Recommended

There are many species, hybrids and cultivars of clematis, but *C.* x *jackmanii* (Jackman clematis) is one of the most popular and hardy vining clematis that blooms in mid- to late summer. The twining vines of this hybrid grow about 10' tall. Large, purple flowers appear on the side shoots from the previous season and on new growth for most of summer.

C. terniflora (sweet autumn clematis; *C. maximowicziana*) is a deciduous or semi-evergreen climber with deep green, lush foliage. It is a later bloomer that bears fragrant, star-shaped, white flowers in late summer, followed by decorative seedheads. (Zones 4–9)

Features: twining habit; early- to late-summer flowers; decorative seedheads **Flower color:** blue, purple, pink, yellow, red, white **Height:** 10–17' or more **Spread:** 5' or more **Hardiness:** zones 3–8

Climbing Hydrangea
Hydrangea

H. aromala subsp. *petiolaris* (above & below)

A mature, climbing hydrangea can cover an entire wall. With its dark, glossy leaves and delicate, lacy flowers, it is quite possibly one of the most stunning climbing plants available.

Growing
Climbing hydrangea prefers **partial shade** or **light shade** but tolerates full sun or full shade. The soil should be of **average to high fertility, humus rich, moist** and **well drained**. This plant performs best in cool, moist conditions, so be sure to mulch its roots.

Climbing hydrangea produces the most flowers when exposed to some direct sunlight each day. It takes time to become established, but it is worth the wait.

Tips
Climbing hydrangea climbs up trees, walls, fences, pergolas and arbors. It clings to walls by means of aerial roots, and therefore needs no support other than a somewhat textured surface. It also grows over rocks and can be used as a ground-cover or trained to form a small tree or shrub.

Recommended
H. anomala subsp. *petiolaris* (*H. petiolaris*) is a clinging, deciduous vine with dark, glossy, green leaves that sometimes turn an attractive yellow in fall. For more than a month in mid-summer, the vine is covered with white, lacy-looking flowers, and the entire plant appears to be veiled in a lacy mist in June.

Features: flowers; clinging habit; exfoliating bark **Flower color:** white **Height:** 50–80' **Spread:** 50–80' **Hardiness:** zones 4–8

Hardy Kiwi
Actinidia

Hardy kiwi is handsome in its simplicity, and its lush green leaves, vigor and adaptability make it very useful, especially on difficult sites.

Growing

Hardy kiwi vines grow best in **full sun**, but they tolerate light shade, resulting in reduced fruit production and less foliage variegation. The soil should be **fertile** and **well drained**. These plants require shelter from strong winds. Protect them from cats until they are established; the hardy kiwi's sap sometimes produces a catnip-like effect on cats.

Tips

These vines need sturdy structures to twine around. Pergolas, arbors or sufficiently large, sturdy fences provide good support. Given a trellis against a wall, a tree or some other upright structure, hardy kiwis will twine upward all summer. They can also be grown in containers.

Hardy kiwi vines can grow uncontrollably. Prune them back if they are getting out of hand. Fruit production is increased by pruning kiwi vines in the same way as grape vines.

Recommended

There are two hardy kiwi vines commonly grown in Iowa gardens. *A. arguta* (hardy kiwi, bower actinidia) has dark green, heart-shaped leaves, white flowers and smooth-skinned, greenish yellow, edible fruit.

A. kolomikta (above), *A. arguta* (below)

A. kolomikta (variegated kiwi vine, kolomikta actinidia) has green leaves strongly variegated with pink and white, smooth-skinned, greenish yellow, edible fruit and white flowers.

Because both a male and a female vine must be present for fruit to be produced, these plants are often sold in pairs.

Features: early-summer flowers; edible fruit; twining habit **Flower color:** white
Height: 15–30' to indefinite
Spread: 15–30' to indefinite
Hardiness: zones 3–8

Honeysuckle

Lonicera

L. *sempervirens* (above), L. x *heckrotii* (below)

Tips

Honeysuckle can be trained to grow up a trellis, fence, arbor or other structure. In a large container near a porch it will ramble over the edges of the pot and up the railings with reckless abandon.

Recommended

There are dozens of honeysuckle species, hybrids and cultivars. Check with your local garden center to see what is available. The following are a few popular hybrids and species.

L. x *heckrotii* is a semi-evergreen, twining climber with sparsely spaced, deep green leaves with a touch of blue. Exotic, fragrant flowers emerge with pink on the outside and orange-yellow on the inside. The flowers are sometimes followed by berries. Cultivars are available with flowers in brighter shades. (Zones 5–9)

oneysuckle can be a rampant, twining vine, but with careful consideration and placement, it won't overrun your garden. The fragrance of the flowers makes any effort worthwhile.

Growing

Honeysuckle grows well in **full sun** or **partial shade**. The soil should be **average to fertile, humus rich, moist** and **well drained**.

L. japonica (Japanese honeysuckle) is a vigorous, semi-evergreen, twining climber covered in dark green foliage and fragrant flowers. Tubular, clustered flowers emerge in white, flushed with purple. Many cultivars are available in a variety of colors and mature sizes.

L. periclymenum (common honeysuckle, woodbine) is another vigorous, twining climber that bears scented, tubular, white to yellow flowers flushed with red in mid- to late summer. Bicolored, streaked and bold-colored cultivars are available. (Zones 5–9)

L. sempervirens (trumpet honeysuckle, coral honeysuckle) bears orange or red flowers in late spring and early summer. Many cultivars and hybrids are available. (Zones 4–8)

Features: late-spring and early-summer flowers; twining habit; fruit **Flower color:** orange, red, pink, white, yellow, bicolored **Height:** 6–15' **Spread:** 6–15' **Hardiness:** zones 4–10

Hyacinth Bean

Lablab (Dolichos)

Using hyacinth bean plants and six to eight bamboo poles that are 6' tall, you can create a living teepee—the perfect hiding place! It's sure to bring a smile to a child's face.

Growing

Hyacinth bean prefers **full sun**. The soil should be **fertile, moist** and **well drained**.

Tips

Hyacinth bean needs a trellis, net, pole or other structure to twine up. Plant it against a fence or near a balcony. If you grow it as a groundcover, make sure it doesn't engulf smaller plants.

Recommended

L. purpureus (*Dolichos lablab*) is a vigorously twining vine. It can grow up to 30' tall, but when grown as an annual, it grows about 10–15' tall. It bears many purple or white flowers over summer, followed by deep purple pods.

L. purpureus (above & below)

The raw beans contain a cyanide-releasing chemical, so never eat the bean. The purple pods are edible if thoroughly cooked with two to four changes of water.

Also called: Egyptian bean, lablab bean, lablab, Indian bean
Features: large, bold leaves; habit; sweet-pea–like flowers
Flower color: purple, white; also grown for purple pods
Height: 10–15' **Spread:** variable **Hardiness:** grown as an annual

Morning Glory

Ipomoea

Morning glory will embellish a chain-link fence, a wire topiary structure or any object thin enough for it to twine its tendrils around. Once established, stand back—this vine grows fast.

Growing

Grow morning glory in **full sun** in **light, well-drained** soil of **poor fertility**. It tolerates any type of soil. Soak seeds for 24 hours before sowing. Start seeds in individual peat pots if sowing indoors. Plant in late spring.

Tips

Morning glory can be grown anywhere: on fences, walls, trees, trellises or arbors. As a groundcover, it will cover any obstacle it encounters.

This vine must twine around objects, such as wire or twine, in order to climb. However, wide fence posts, walls or other broad objects are too large.

Recommended

I. alba (moonflower) has sweetly scented, white flowers that open at night.

I. purpurea (common morning glory) bears trumpet-shaped flowers in purple, blue, pink or white.

I. tricolor (morning glory) produces purple or blue flowers with white centers. Many cultivars are available.

I. alba (above), *I. tricolor* (below)

Each morning glory flower lasts for only one day. The buds form a spiral that slowly unfurls as the day brightens with the rising sun.

Features: fast growth **Flower color:** white, blue, pink, purple, variegated **Height:** 10–12' **Spread:** 12–24" **Hardiness:** annual

Porcelain Berry
Ampelopsis

This vine has attractive foliage, colorful berries, a reliable and vigorous growth habit and incredible fall color. Finally, a vine that has it all—year-round interest.

Growing

Porcelain berry requires **full to partial sun** in **moist** but **well-drained** soil. Prune after flowering if flowering on the previous year's growth, or from late winter to spring if flowering on the current year's growth.

Tips

Porcelain berry is ideal for climbing up a trellis, arbor or pergola. Because of its vigorous growth habit, this vine can cover a wall, fence or old tree in no time at all.

Recommended

A. brevipedunculata is a vigorous climbing vine. The leaves are large and resemble grape leaves. Clusters of small, green flowers emerge in summer, followed by green berries that change to light blue and finally to purple. '**Elegans**' is a little less vigorous than the species, and it produces dark green foliage with mottled white and pink markings.

A. brevipedunculata (above & below)

Porcelain berry is often grown for its attractive foliage, which turns a stunning shade of red and yellow in the cool days of fall.

Features: colorful berry clusters; ornate foliage and habit **Height:** 10–15'
Spread: variable **Hardiness:** zones 5–8

Wisteria

Wisteria

'Aunt Dee' (above)

Loose, purple clusters hang like lace from the branches of wisteria.

Growing

Wisteria grows well in **full sun** or **partial shade**. The soil should be of **average fertility, moist** and **well drained**. Wisteria grown in too fertile a soil will produce a lot of vegetative growth but very few flowers. Avoid planting wisteria near a lawn where fertilizer may leach into the vine's root zone.

All parts of this plant, including the seeds in the long, velvety, bean-like pods, are poisonous.

Tips

Wisteria requires something to twine around, such as an arbor or other sturdy structure. You can also stake a wisteria and train it to form a small tree. Try to select a permanent site for your wisteria; it doesn't like to be moved. This vigorous vine may send up suckers and can root wherever its branches touch the ground. Frequent pruning is required to control this vine and keep it looking its best.

Recommended

W. macrostachya (Kentucky wisteria, native American wisteria) is a hardy vine that produces lilac-purple, pendulous, egg-shaped clusters of flowers 8–12" long on woody, twining stems. This species is much less vigorous than other species but is more tolerant of wet soils. The flowers have a subtle fragrance, though less so than their oriental counterparts, and they bloom later, when the leaves are already on the plants. Its presentation is certainly less dramatic than more tender species, but it offers an understated elegance. '**Aunt Dee**' bears light purple flower clusters early in the season. '**Clara Mack**' is considered to be the showiest of several introduced varieties. It bears longer, white flower clusters in June and July and may bloom again later in the season.

Features: late-spring flowers; foliage; twining habit
Flower color: white, blue, purple, pink **Height:** 15–25'
or more **Spread:** 15–25' or more **Hardiness:** zones 4–8

Allium

Allium

A. giganteum (above), *A. cernuum* (below)

Allium, with its striking, ball-like or loose, nodding clusters of flowers, is sure to attract attention in the garden.

Growing

Allium grows best in **full sun**. The soil should be **average to fertile, moist** and **well drained**. Plant the bulbs in fall.

Tips

Allium is more attractive in groups in a bed or border where it can be left to naturalize. Most allium plants will self-seed when left to their own devices. The foliage, which tends to fade just as the plants come into flower, can be hidden with groundcover or a low, bushy companion plant.

After allium blooms, leave the flowerheads to dry on the stems. The dry flowers provide a starry feature all summer long.

Recommended

Several allium species, hybrids and cultivars have gained popularity for their decorative flowers. *A. aflatunense* has dense, globe-like clusters of lavender flowers. *A. caeruleum* (blue globe onion) bears globe-like clusters of blue flowers. *A. cernuum* (nodding or wild onion) has loose, drooping clusters of pink flowers. *A. giganteum* (giant onion) is a towering plant with large, globe-shaped clusters of pinky purple flowers. *A. sphaerocephalon* (drumstick allium) bears reddish purple, egg-shaped, tightly packed flower clusters atop wiry stems.

Although its leaves have an onion scent when bruised, the flowers have a sweeter fragrance.

Features: summer flowers; cylindrical or strap-shaped leaves **Flower color:** pink, purple, white, yellow, blue, maroon **Height:** 1–4' **Spread:** 2–12" **Hardiness:** zones 3–8

Caladium

Caladium

'Red Flash' (above), 'White Queen' (below)

The midribs and veining of caladium's striking foliage only strengthen the combinations, helping to draw the eye to the smashing leaf colors. If you are searching for bold texture in the garden, caladium is a must.

Growing

Caladium prefers to grow in **partial to full shade** in **moist, well-drained, humus-rich, slightly acidic** soil.

Caladium is a tuberous plant that can be grown from seed or from the tuber. Start growing the tuber indoors in a soil-less planting mix, with a minimum soil temperature of 70° F. Once it has leafed-out, the tuber can handle a cooler soil temperature

of minimum 55° F. When planting out, add a little bonemeal or fishmeal to the planting hole. Make sure the knobby side of the tuber is facing up and is level with the soil surface or just under.

Dig tubers in fall after the leaves die back. Remove as much soil as possible and let the tubers dry for a few days. Store them in slightly damp peat moss at 55–60° F. Tubers can be divided in spring before planting. Divisions of tubers are more subject to fungal diseases owing to the newly exposed surfaces.

Tips

Caladium is an excellent plant for giving your garden a tropical feel. It does very well around water features and in woodland gardens. It is equally effective in a herbaceous border in masses or as specimens, and it is a wonderful container plant. When caladium is grown in a container, there is no need to dig up the tuber in fall; simply bring the whole container inside over winter.

All parts of caladium may irritate the skin, and ingesting this plant will cause stomach upset.

Recommended

C. x *hortulanum* (*C. bicolor*) is native to the edge of woodlands in tropical South America. The often tufted, arrow-shaped foliage is dark green and variously marked and patterned with red, white, pink, green, rose, salmon, silver or bronze. Each leaf is 6–12" long.

Also called: elephant's ears, heart-of-Jesus, mother-in-law plant, angel wings
Features: ornate, patterned and colorful foliage; habit; form **Flower color:** greenish white; plants grown for foliage **Height:** 18–24"
Spread: 18–24" **Hardiness:** treat as an annual

Calla Lily

Zantedeschia

This beautiful, exotic-looking plant was only available as a cut flower in the past. The introduction of new cultivars, however, has made it more readily available and worth planting.

Growing

Calla lilies grow best in **full sun**. The soil should be **fertile, humus rich** and **moist**. Calla lilies grown in containers can be brought indoors over winter. Reduce watering in winter, keeping the soil just moist.

Tips

Calla lilies are ideal additions to mixed beds and borders, and they work well as container specimens. They are also a great addition to a water garden, as they grow and thrive in wet locations and can even be partially submerged in shallow water.

Rather than moving large, cumbersome plants, it is sometimes easier to remove small divisions in fall and transfer them indoors over winter.

Recommended

Z. aethiopica (white arum lily, white calla) forms a clump of arrow-shaped, glossy green leaves. It bears white flowers from late spring to mid-summer. Several cultivars are available.

Although they grow quite large, calla lilies can be grown as houseplants year-round, but they benefit from spending summer outdoors.

Z. aethiopica (above), *Z. elliottiana* cultivar (below)

Z. elliottiana (yellow calla, golden calla) forms a basal clump of white-spotted, dark green, heart-shaped leaves. It grows 24–36" tall and spreads 8–12". This species bears yellow, red, orange and pink flowers in summer and is a parent plant of many popular hybrids.

Features: flowers; foliage **Flower color:** yellow, white **Height:** 16–36" **Spread:** 8–24" **Hardiness:** treat as an annual

Canna Lily

Canna

Canna lilies are stunning, dramatic plants that give an exotic flair to any garden.

Growing

Canna lilies grow best in **full sun** in a **sheltered** location. The soil should be **fertile, moist** and **well drained**. Plant out in spring, once the soil has warmed. Canna lilies can be started early indoors in containers to get a head start on the growing season. Deadhead to prolong blooming.

Tips

Canna lilies can be grown in a bed or border. They make dramatic specimen plants and can even be included in large planters.

Recommended

A wide range of canna lilies are available, including cultivars and hybrids with green, bronzy, purple or yellow-and-green-striped foliage. Flowers may be white, red, orange, pink, yellow or bicolored. Dwarf cultivars that grow 18–28" tall are also available.

C. 'Red King Humbert' (below)

Canna lily rhizomes can be lifted after the foliage is killed back in fall. Clean off any clinging dirt and store them in a cool, frost-free location in slightly moist peat moss. Check on them regularly through winter and, if they start to sprout, pot them and move them to a bright window until they can be moved outdoors.

Features: decorative foliage; summer flowers
Flower color: white, red, orange, pink, yellow, bicolored **Height:** 3–6' **Spread:** 20–36"
Hardiness: grown as an annual

Crocus

Crocus

C. x *vernus* (above & below)

rocuses are harbingers of spring. They often appear, as if by magic, in full bloom from beneath the melting snow.

Growing

Crocuses grow well in **full sun** or **light, dappled shade**. The soil should be of **poor to average fertility, gritty** and **well drained**. Plant the corms about 4" deep in fall. Foliage should be left in place after the plants flower but can be cut back once it begins to wither and turn brown in summer.

Tips

Crocuses are almost always planted in groups. Drifts of crocuses can be planted in lawns to provide interest and color while the grass still lies dormant. After the foliage withers in mid-June, crocuses may be mowed over. In beds and borders they can be left to naturalize. Groups of plants will fill in and spread out to provide a bright welcome in spring. Plant perennials among the crocuses to fill in the gaps once the crocuses fade away.

Recommended

Many crocus species, hybrids and cultivars are available. The spring-flowering crocus most people are familiar with is *C.* x *vernus*, commonly called Dutch crocus. Many cultivars are available, with flowers in shades of purple, yellow and white, sometimes bicolored or with darker veins.

Crocuses bloom in spring or fall, are hardy to zone 5 and can be grown successfully in warmer areas of Iowa. Cold-treated bulbs can be planted in spring in colder areas.

Features: early-spring flowers
Flower color: purple, yellow, white, bicolored **Height:** 2–6"
Spread: 2–4"
Hardiness: zones 3–8

Daffodil

Narcissus

When they think of daffodils, many gardeners automatically think of large, yellow, trumpet-shaped flowers, but there is a lot of variety in color, form and size among daffodils.

Growing

Daffodils grow best in **full sun** or **light, dappled shade**. The soil should be **average to fertile, moist** and **well drained**. Bulbs should be planted in fall, 4–8" deep, depending on the size of the bulb. The bigger the bulb, the deeper it should be planted. A rule of thumb is to measure the bulb from top to bottom and multiply that number by three to know how deeply to plant.

The cup in the center of a daffodil is called the corona, and the group of petals that surrounds the corona is called the perianth.

Tips

Daffodils are often planted where they can be left to naturalize, in the light shade beneath a tree or in a woodland garden. In mixed beds and borders, the faded leaves are hidden by the summer foliage of other plants.

Recommended

Many species, hybrids and cultivars of daffodils are available. Flowers come in shades of white, yellow, peach, orange and pink, and may be bicolored. Flowers may be 1½–6" across, solitary or borne in clusters. There are 12 flower-form categories.

Features: spring flowers
Flower color: white, yellow, peach, orange, pink, bicolored **Height:** 4–24"
Spread: 14–12" **Hardiness:** zones 3–8

Frittilary

Frittillaria

Frittilary plants will offer a formal element to an otherwise casual setting, bearing the most unusual, royal-looking blossoms in early summer.

Growing

Frittilary prefers **full sun** or **light shade** in an area sheltered from the wind. The soil should be **coarse, organically rich, moist** and very **well drained.** It is important that the soil not be allowed to dry out during its dormant period in the midst of the growing season.

To protect frittilary bulbs from late-spring frosts, plant them up to 9" or more deep, and at least 4" apart from one another. These plants can be further propagated by division, offsets and seed.

Tips

There are many frittilary species to choose from, but crown imperial frittilary can grow quite tall and has the most architectural appeal. These flowers are most striking planted in large groupings at the back of mixed borders, where the scent may be a little less evident. Frittilaries are also best grown among shrubbery; they won't be disturbed and will benefit from fallen leaf matter, both as a mulch and organic matter.

Recommended

F. imperialis (crown imperial frittilary) is a true bulb that produces a lush cluster of blade-like leaves at the base of a tall, slender stalk. The stalk is bare up to the top, where a large cluster of pendent, bell-shaped blossoms surround the tip, topped with a further cluster of green foliage. Many cultivars are available in fiery shades of orange, yellow and red.

Clumps of frittilary are quite stunning among groupings of ornamental grasses for naturalizing, or in an established garden that is rarely disturbed and settled.

Frittilary bulbs are a great deterrent to rodents and deer.

Features: striking, pendent flowers in early to mid-summer; form **Flower color:** orange, yellow, red **Height:** 3–4' **Spread:** 6–12" **Hardiness:** zones 4–8

Gladiolus

Gladiolus

'Homecoming' (below)

Perhaps best known as a cut flower, gladiolus adds an air of extravagance to the garden.

Growing

Gladiolus grows best in **full sun** but tolerates partial shade. The soil should be **fertile, humus rich, moist** and **well drained**. Flower spikes may need staking and shelter from wind to prevent them from blowing over.

Plant corms in spring, 4–6" deep, once soil has warmed. Corms can also be started early indoors. Plant a few corms each week for about a month to prolong the blooming period.

Tips

Planted in groups in beds and borders, gladiolus makes a bold statement. Corms can also be pulled up in fall and stored in damp peat moss in a cool, frost-free location over winter.

Recommended

G. x *hortulanus* is a huge group of hybrids. Gladiolus flowers come in almost every imaginable shade, except blue. Plants are commonly grouped in three classifications: **Grandiflorus** is the best known, each corm producing a single spike of large, often ruffled flowers; **Nanus**, the hardiest group, survives in zone 3 with protection and produces several spikes of up to seven flowers; and **Primulinus** produces a single spike of up to 23 flowers that grows more spaced out than those of Grandiflorus.

Features: brightly colored mid- to late-summer flowers
Flower color: all colors, except blue **Height:** 18"–6'
Spread: 6–12" **Hardiness:** zone 8; grown as an annual

Grape Hyacinth
Muscari

Tulips should never be alone to signal the emergence of spring. Grape hyacinth bulbs are the perfect accompaniment and contrast beautifully with just about any color combination.

Growing

Grape hyacinth prefers **full sun to partial shade**. The soil should be **well drained** and **organically rich**.

Tips

Grape hyacinth bulbs are great for naturalizing. Plant individual bulbs random distances from one another in your lawn, but don't plan on cutting the grass until the grape hyacinth leaves have died down for another year. This flower looks quite beautiful planted with perennials, which will slowly envelop the tired-looking grape hyacinth foliage as they grow to their full size for the season. The leaves of grape hyacinths emerge in fall and are often planted around other bulbs as markers, to ensure that they aren't forgotten about and dug up.

Recommended

M. armeniacum (Armenian grape hyacinth) is the most well-known species. It produces grass-like foliage and clusters of purple blue, grape-like flowers atop slender green stems. The flowers emit a strong, musky scent.

M. botryoides (common grape hyacinth) is very similar in appearance in a slightly more compact form.

M. armeniacum (above & below)

It is less invasive than other species and will naturalize in a more respectable manner.

M. latifolium (bicolor muscari, giant grape hyacinth, one-leaf hyacinth) is a taller species that blooms a little later than the other species. It bears broader leaves and bicolored blooms. From each flower spike emerges two different kinds of flowers—smaller, sterile flowers in light blue towards the tip and darker, fertile flowers further down.

Grape hyacinths are a welcome sight in the early months of spring, soon after the first raft of spring bulbs has emerged.

Features: grape-like clusters of fragrant flowers; habit **Flower color:** purple, blue **Height:** 6–10" **Spread:** 6–8" **Hardiness:** zones 2–8

Hyacinth

Hyacinthus

The fragrance from one flower is powerful but intoxicating when planted en masse.

Growing

Hyacinth requires a location in **full sun** for the best results. The soil should be **moist, well drained** and **rich in organic matter.** Hot and dry locations aren't recommended. Plant the bulbs 6–8" deep and 2–3" apart from one another. For a more naturalistic effect, plant them in odd numbers and groupings rather than in rows.

Hyacinth bulbs should be planted in fall for spring blooming. They require at least four to six weeks to develop an adequate root system. This should take place before the ground has a chance to freeze. Ensure that the newly planted bulbs have adequate water before the ground freezes.

Tips

Hyacinth bulbs are often planted among perennials and shrubbery, which emerge earlier in spring. Once hyacinth flowers begin to fade, the newly emerging plants surrounding the bulbs will soon obscure the fading hyacinth foliage. The purple, pink and white flowers are a lovely complement to other flowering bulbs, including daffodils, tulips and crocuses. Hyacinth bulbs are easy to force indoors, providing a fragrant, floral display.

Recommended

There are a vast array of hyacinth cultivars to choose from, including single and double flowering types, ranging in every shade of purple, blue, white and pink that you can imagine. They're also available in different sizes and flowering periods, including early-, mid- and late-spring bloom times. Consult your local garden center for the best recommendations and availability.

Features: fragrant, colorful flowers; lengthy bloom time **Flower color:** purple, blue, pink, white, cream **Height:** 10" **Spread:** 4–6" **Hardiness:** zones 5–7

Lily

Lilium

'Stargazer' (below)

Decorative clusters of large, richly colored blooms grace these tall plants. Flowers are produced at different times of the season, depending on the hybrid, and it is possible to have lilies blooming all season if a variety of cultivars are chosen.

Growing

Lilies grow best in **full sun** but like to have their **roots shaded**. The soil should be rich in **organic matter, fertile, moist** and **well drained**.

Tips

Lilies are often grouped in beds and borders and can be naturalized in woodland gardens and near water features. These plants are narrow but tall; group at least three plants together to create some volume.

Recommended

The many species, hybrids and cultivars available are grouped by type. Visit your local garden center to see what is available. The following are two popular groups of lilies. **Asiatic hybrids** bear clusters of flowers in early summer or mid-summer and are available in a wide range of colors. **Oriental hybrids** bear clusters of large, fragrant flowers in mid- and late summer. Colors are usually white, pink or red.

Also called: Oriental lily, Asiatic lily
Features: early-, mid- or late-summer flowers
Flower color: orange, yellow, peach, pink, purple, red, white **Height:** 2–5' **Spread:** 12"
Hardiness: zones 2–8

Snowdrop

Galanthus

Galanthus species with *Eranthis hyemalis* (above), *G. nivalis* (below)

If winter has you feeling dull and dreary, let early-blooming snowdrops bring some much-needed color to your winter garden.

Growing

Snowdrops grow well in **full sun to partial shade** in **fertile, well-drained, moist, humus-rich** soil. Do not allow the soil to dry out in summer.

All parts of snowdrops are poisonous if ingested. Handling the bulbs may cause some irritation for people with sensitive skin.

Tips

Snowdrops work well in beds, borders and rock gardens. Snowdrops should always be planted in groups and close to one another for the best effect. They can be planted in the lawn or under deciduous shrubs and trees that will provide partial shade in summer. Snowdrops are great for naturalizing in lightly shaded woodlands.

Recommended

G. nivalis (common snowdrop) is a tiny plant that produces small, nodding, honey-scented, white flowers in mid- to late winter. The inner petals are marked with a green 'V' shape. Cultivars are available, some with double flowers and some with yellow markings instead of green.

The various snowdrop species hybridize easily with one another; many hybrids are available.

Features: early-blooming flowers; strap-like foliage; easy to grow **Flower color:** white **Height:** 4–12" **Spread:** 4–6" **Hardiness:** zones 3–8

Siberian Squill
Scilla

It should be no surprise that this bulb is extremely hardy based on its name. Its delicate and dainty appearance may fool some, but Siberian squill will soon prove its worthiness in the Iowa landscape.

Growing

Siberian squill will grow in full sun but prefers **partial shade**. The soil should be **rich** and **sandy**, but this plant tolerates a wide variety of soils as long as it's very **well drained**.

Plant the bulbs soon after purchase because they do not store well and may dry out. It's also beneficial for the bulbs to be well established before the onset of winter. The bulbs should be planted at least 3" deep and 1–2" apart from one another.

Tips

Siberian squill is most effective when planted in large groupings. It is ideal for areas that require a subtle touch of color low to the ground. Naturalized areas will also benefit from random plantings of this flowering bulb, adding a hint of color in a meadow-like setting. Siberian squill is also good for forcing indoors.

Recommended

S. siberica produces a cluster of narrow, blade-like foliage. Three to four stems emerge through the center of the crown, bearing nodding, bell-shaped flowers. Cultivars and varieties are available in different sizes and flower colors.

Siberian squill is often one of the first flowering bulbs to bloom in spring and is incredibly hardy and tolerant of adverse conditions.

Features: dainty flowers; habit; hardiness; tolerant of poor conditions **Flower color:** white, blue, purple **Height:** 2–4" **Spread:** 2–3" **Hardiness:** zones 1–8

Tulip

Tulipa

Tulips, with their beautiful, often garishly colored flowers, are a welcome sight in the warm days of spring.

Growing

Tulips grow best in **full sun**. The flowers tend to bend toward the light in light or partial shade. The soil should be **fertile** and **well drained**. Plant bulbs in fall, 4–6" deep, depending on size of bulb. Bulbs that have been cold treated can be planted in spring. Although tulips can repeat bloom, many hybrids perform best if planted new each year. Species and older cultivars are the best choice for naturalizing.

Tips

Tulips provide the best display when mass planted or planted in groups in flowerbeds and borders. They can also be grown in containers and can be forced to bloom early in pots indoors. Some of the species and older cultivars can be naturalized in meadow and wildflower gardens.

Recommended

There are about 100 species of tulips and thousands of hybrids and cultivars. They are generally divided into 15 groups based on bloom time and flower appearance. They come in dozens of shades, with many bicolored or multi-colored varieties. Blue is the only shade not available. Check with your local garden center in early fall for the best selection.

During the 'tulipomania' of the 1630s, the bulbs were worth many times their weight in gold, and many tulip speculators lost massive fortunes when the mania ended.

Features: spring flowers **Flower color:** all colors, except blue **Height:** 6–30" **Spread:** 2–8" **Hardiness:** zones 3–8

Basil
Ocimum

The sweet, fragrant leaves of fresh basil add a delicious, licorice-like flavor to salads and tomato-based dishes.

Growing

Basil grows best in a **warm, sheltered** location in **full sun**. The soil should be **fertile, moist** and **well drained**. Pinch tips regularly to encourage bushy growth. Plant out or direct sow seed after frost danger has passed in spring.

Tips

Although basil will grow best in a warm spot outdoors in the garden, it can be grown successfully in a pot by a bright window indoors to provide you with fresh leaves all year.

Recommended

O. basilicum is one of the most popular of the culinary herbs. There are dozens of varieties, including ones with large or tiny, green or purple and smooth or ruffled leaves.

'Genovese' (above), 'Red Rubin' (below)

Basil is a good companion plant for tomatoes—both like warm, moist growing conditions—and when you pick tomatoes for a salad you'll also remember to include a few leaves of basil.

Features: fragrant, decorative leaves
Height: 12–24" **Spread:** 18"
Hardiness: tender annual

Borage
Borago

Borage is a vigorous, tenacious annual herb. It is valued by some but disliked by others because of its natural inclination to reseed itself everywhere. The flowers and foliage are not only pretty but are also useful in salads and desserts.

Growing
Borage prefers **full sun** and **moist, sandy, well-drained** soil. Borage is drought tolerant once established. Remove any unwanted seedlings as they emerge in early spring to prevent an onslaught of plants.

Tips
Plant borage in your vegetable or herb garden to attract bees for pollination. As an ornamental, borage contrasts beautifully with dark foliage specimens.

Recommended
B. officinalis is an upright plant with high clusters of pendent, violet blue flowers in spring. The stems and foliage are covered in silvery hairs that complement the bluish flowers.

B. officinalis (above & below)

Young leaves are yummy in cool, raw salads, cold summer drinks or cooked with vegetables. The flowers can be candied for decorating desserts.

Features: flowers; habit; fuzzy foliage and stems **Flower color:** violet blue
Height: 24–36" **Spread:** 24"
Hardiness: zones 5–10

Chives

Allium

The delicate onion flavor of chives is best enjoyed fresh. Mix chives into dips or sprinkle them on salads and baked potatoes.

Growing

Chives grow best in **full sun**. The soil should be **fertile, moist** and **well drained**, but chives adapt to most soil conditions. These plants are easy to start from seed, but they do like the soil temperature to stay above 66° F before they will germinate, so seeds started directly in the garden are unlikely to sprout before early summer.

Tips

Chives are decorative enough to be included in a mixed or herbaceous border and can be left to naturalize. In an herb garden, chives should be given plenty of space to allow self-seeding.

A. schoenoprasum (above & below)

Recommended

A. schoenoprasum forms a clump of bright green, cylindrical leaves. Clusters of pinky purple flowers are produced in early and mid-summer. Varieties with white or pink flowers are available.

Chives are said to increase appetite and encourage good digestion.

Features: foliage; form; flowers **Flower color:** pinky purple, white, pink **Height:** 8–24" **Spread:** 12" or more **Hardiness:** zones 3–8

Coriander · Cilantro

Coriandrum

C. sativum (above & below)

Coriander is a multi-purpose herb. The leaves are called cilantro and are used in salads, salsas and soups; the seeds are called coriander and are used in pies, chutneys and marmalades.

Growing

Coriander prefers **full sun** but tolerates partial shade. The soil should be **fertile, light** and **well drained**. These plants dislike humid conditions and do best during a dry summer.

Tips

Coriander has pungent leaves and is best planted where people will not have to brush past it. It is, however, a delight to behold when in flower. Add a plant or two here and there throughout your borders and vegetable garden, both for the visual appeal and to attract beneficial insects.

Recommended

C. sativum forms a clump of lacy, basal foliage above which large, loose clusters of tiny, white flowers are produced. The seeds ripen in late summer and fall.

The delicate, cloud-like cluster of white flowers attracts pollinating insects, such as butterflies and bees, as well as abundant predatory insects that will help keep pest insects at a minimum in your garden.

Features: form; foliage; flowers; seeds **Flower color:** white
Height: 16–24" **Spread:** 8–16" **Hardiness:** tender annual

Dill
Anethum

Dill leaves and seeds are probably best known for their use as pickling herbs, though they have a wide variety of other culinary uses.

Growing

Dill grows best in **full sun** in a **sheltered** location out of strong winds. The soil should be of **poor to average fertility, moist** and **well drained**. Sow seeds every couple of weeks in spring and early summer to ensure a regular supply of leaves.

Dill should not be planted near fennel because they will cross-pollinate and the seeds will lose their distinct flavors.

Tips

With its feathery leaves, dill is an attractive addition to a mixed bed or border. It can be included in a vegetable garden but does well in any sunny location. Dill also attracts predatory insects to the garden.

A. graveolens (above & below)

Recommended

A. graveolens forms a clump of feathery foliage. Clusters of yellow flowers are borne at the tops of sturdy stems.

Dill turns up frequently in historical records as both a culinary and a medicinal herb. It was used by the Egyptians and Romans and is mentioned in the Bible.

Features: feathery, edible foliage; flowers; edible seeds **Flower color:** yellow **Height:** 2–5' **Spread:** 12" or more **Hardiness:** annual

Lemon Verbena
Aloysia

A. triphylla (above & below)

Lemon verbena has a wide variety of uses. Its fresh leaves can be used to flavor oils, vinegars, drinks, desserts, stuffings and fragrant sachets for year-round enjoyment.

Growing
Lemon verbena prefers a **sunny** location. The soil should be **light, well drained** and **fertile**.

Tips
Lemon verbena is a half-hardy perennial, best grown in a container in colder regions so it can be brought inside over winter. It also works well in a formal herb or medicinal garden.

Recommended
A. triphylla produces pale green, narrow leaves that smell strongly of lemon. Tiny, white flowers tinged with pale purple emerge in early summer.

Aloysia was named after the Princess of Parma, Maria Louisa, who died in 1819. Lemon verbena was commonly known as 'the lemon plant' in the Victorian era.

Features: aromatic foliage
Flower color: white tinged with pale purple **Height:** 3–4' **Spread:** 18–36"
Hardiness: half-hardy perennial

Mint

Mentha

The cool, refreshing flavor of mint lends itself to tea and other hot or cold beverages. Mint sauce, made from freshly chopped mint leaves, is often served with lamb.

Growing

Mint grows well in **full sun** or **partial shade**. The soil should be **average to fertile, humus rich** and **moist**. These plants spread vigorously by rhizomes and will need a barrier in the soil to restrict their spread.

Tips

Mint is a good groundcover for damp spots. It grows well along ditches that may only be periodically wet. It also can be used in beds and borders but may overwhelm less vigorous plants.

The flowers attract bees, butterflies and other pollinators to the garden.

Recommended

There are many species, hybrids and cultivars of mint. Spearmint (*M. spicata*), peppermint (*M.* x *piperita*) and lemon mint (*M.* x *piperata* 'Citrata') are three of the most commonly grown culinary varieties. There are also more decorative varieties with variegated or curly leaves, as well as varieties with unusual, fruit-scented leaves.

A few sprigs of fresh mint added to a pitcher of iced tea give it an added zip.

Features: fragrant foliage; flowers
Flower color: purple, pink, white **Height:** 6–36"
Spread: 36" or more **Hardiness:** zones 4–8

Oregano · Marjoram
Origanum

Oregano and marjoram are two of the best known and most frequently used herbs. They are popular in stuffings, soups and stews—and no pizza is complete until it has been sprinkled with fresh or dried oregano leaves.

Growing
Oregano and marjoram grow best in **full sun**. The soil should be of **poor to average fertility, neutral to alkaline** and **well drained**. The flowers attract pollinators to the garden.

Tips
These bushy perennials make a lovely addition to any border and can be trimmed to form low hedges.

Recommended
O. majorana (marjoram) is upright and shrubby with light green, hairy leaves. It bears white or pink flowers in summer and can be grown as an annual where it is not hardy.

O. vulgare 'Polyphant' (above), *O. vulgare* 'Aureum' (below)

In Greek, oros *means 'mountain' and* ganos *means 'joy and beauty,' so* oregano *translates as 'joy or beauty of the mountain.'*

O. vulgare var. **hirtum** (oregano, Greek oregano) is the most flavorful culinary variety of oregano. The low, bushy plant has hairy, gray-green leaves and bears white flowers. Many other interesting varieties of *O. vulgare* are available, including those with golden, variegated or curly leaves.

Features: fragrant foliage; flowers; bushy habit
Flower color: white, pink **Height:** 12–32"
Spread: 8–18" **Hardiness:** zones 5–8

Parsley

Petroselinum

P. crispum (above & below)

Although usually used as a garnish, parsley is rich in vitamins and minerals and is reputed to freshen the breath after garlic- or onion-rich foods are eaten.

Growing

Parsley grows well in **full sun** or **partial shade**. The soil should be of **average to rich fertility, humus rich, moist** and **well drained**. Direct sow seeds because the plants resent transplanting. If you start seeds early, use peat pots so the plants can be potted or planted out without disruption.

Tips

Parsley should be started where you plan to grow it. Containers of parsley can be kept close to the house for easy picking. The bright green leaves and compact growth habit make parsley a good edging plant for beds and borders.

Cut up freshly picked parsley leaves and sprinkle them over mixed greens for a tasty and nutritious salad.

Recommended

P. crispum forms a clump of bright green, divided leaves. This plant is biennial, but it is usually grown as an annual. Cultivars may have flat or curly leaves. Flat leaves are more flavorful and curly leaves are more decorative. Dwarf cultivars are also available.

Features: attractive foliage **Height:** 8–24"
Spread: 12–24" **Hardiness:** zones 5–8

Rosemary

Rosmarinus

R. officinalis (above & below)

Rosemary's needle-like leaves are used to flavor a wide variety of culinary dishes, including chicken, pork, lamb, rice, tomato, potato and egg dishes.

To overwinter a container-grown plant, keep it in very light or partial shade in summer, then put it in a sunny window indoors during winter. Keep it well watered but not soaking wet.

Growing

Rosemary prefers **full sun** but tolerates partial shade. The soil should be of **poor to average fertility** and **well drained**. Place rosemary in an area with good air circulation to prevent mildew.

Tips

Grow rosemary in a shrub border where it's hardy. In colder regions, rosemary is usually grown in a container as a specimen or with other plants. Low-growing, spreading plants can be included in a rock garden or along the top of a retaining wall, or they can be grown in hanging baskets and containers. Rosemary plants can also be trained into standard forms and trimmed to form topiary shapes.

Recommended

R. officinalis is a dense, bushy, tender evergreen shrub with narrow, dark green leaves. The habit varies somewhat between cultivars, from strongly upright to prostrate and spreading. Flowers usually come in shades of blue, but pink- or white-flowered cultivars are available. A cultivar called 'Arp' can survive in zone 6 in a sheltered location with winter protection. Plants rarely reach their mature size when grown in containers.

Features: fragrant, evergreen foliage; summer flowers **Flower color:** usually bright blue, sometimes pink or white **Height:** 8"–4' **Spread:** 1–4' **Hardiness:** zone 8

Sage
Salvia

Sage is perhaps best known as a flavoring for stuffings, but it has a great range of uses, including in soups, stews, sausages and dumplings.

Growing

Sage prefers **full sun** but tolerates light shade. The soil should be of **average fertility** and **well drained**. These plants benefit from a light mulch of compost each year. They are drought tolerant once established.

Tips

Sage is an attractive plant for a border, adding volume to the middle of the border or as an attractive edging or feature plant near the front. Sage can also be grown in mixed planters.

Recommended

S. officinalis is a woody, mounding plant with soft, gray-green leaves. Spikes of light purple flowers appear in early and mid-summer. Many cultivars with attractive foliage are available, including the silver-leaved '**Berggarten**,' the purple-leaved '**Purpurea**,' the yellow-margined '**Icterina**,' and the purple-green and cream variegated '**Tricolor**,' whose growth has a pink flush.

'Icterina' (above), 'Purpurea' (below)

Sage has been used since at least ancient Greek times as a medicinal and culinary herb and continues to be widely used for both those purposes today.

Features: fragrant, decorative foliage; summer flowers
Flower color: blue, light purple
Height: 12–24" **Spread:** 18–36"
Hardiness: zones 4–8

Thyme
Thymus

T. vulgaris (above), T. x citriodorus 'Argenteus' (below)

These plants are bee magnets when blooming, and thyme honey is pleasantly herbal and goes very well with biscuits.

Thyme is a popular culinary herb used in soups, stews, casseroles and with roasts.

Growing

Thyme prefers **full sun**. The soil should be **neutral to alkaline** and of **poor to average fertility**. **Good drainage** is essential. It is beneficial to work leaf mold and sharp limestone gravel into the soil to improve structure and drainage.

Tips

Thyme is useful for sunny, dry locations at the front of borders, between or beside paving stones, on rock gardens and rock walls and in containers.

Once the plants have finished flowering, shear them back by about half to encourage new growth and prevent the plants from becoming too woody.

Recommended

T. x *citriodorus* (lemon-scented thyme) forms a mound of lemon-scented, dark green foliage. The flowers are pale pink. Cultivars with silver- or gold-margined leaves are available.

T. vulgaris (common thyme) forms a bushy mound of dark green leaves. The flowers may be purple, pink or white. Cultivars with variegated leaves are available.

Features: bushy habit; fragrant, decorative foliage; flowers **Flower color:** purple, pink, white **Height:** 8–16" **Spread:** 8–16" **Hardiness:** zones 4–8

Blue Fescue

Festuca

F. glauca 'Elijah Blue' (above), *F. glauca* (below)

This fine-leaved ornamental grass forms tufted clumps that resemble pin cushions. Their metallic-blue coloring adds an all-season cooling accent to the garden.

Growing

Fescue thrives in **full sun to light shade**. The soil should be of **average fertility**, **moist** and **well drained**. Plants are drought tolerant once established. Fescue emerges early in spring, so shear it back to 1" above the crown in late winter, before new growth emerges. Shear off flower stalks just above the foliage to keep the plant tidy or to prevent self-seeding.

If you enjoy blue fescue, you might also like the large, coarse-textured, blue oat grass, Helictotrichon sempervirens *'Saphirsprudel' (Sapphire Fountain), which can grow 4' tall when in flower.*

Tips

With its fine texture and distinct blue color, fescue can be used as a single specimen in a rock garden or in a container planting. Plant fescue in drifts to create a sea of blue or a handsome edge to a bed, border or pathway. It looks attractive in both formal and informal gardens.

Recommended

F. glauca (blue fescue) forms tidy, tufted clumps of fine, blue-toned foliage and panicles of flowers in May and June. Cultivars and hybrids come in varying heights and in shades ranging from blue to olive green. 'Elijah Blue,' 'Boulder Blue,' 'Skinner's Blue' and 'Solling' are popular selections.

Features: blue to blue-green foliage that persists into winter; habit **Height:** 6–12" **Spread:** 10–12" **Hardiness:** zones 3–9

Blue Oat Grass

Helictotrichon

H. sempervirens

This hardy grass is the perfect plant for those who desire a super-sized version of blue fescue for their garden.

Growing

Blue oat grass will thrive in a **sunny** location. The soil should be **average to dry** and **well drained**. This grass is considered to be an evergreen but will still need a trim in spring to encourage new growth or to simply tidy it up.

Blue oat grass is easily propagated by division in early spring. It is a cool-season perennial that is a reliable Iowa dweller.

Tips

This large, nonspreading grass is ideal for just about any setting because of its versatility. It would work well in a xeriscape design or naturalized area. It is a lovely complement to flowering perennials and shrubs because of its coloration, overall size and growth habit.

Recommended

H. sempervirens produces perfectly rounded, dome-shaped clumps of intensely blue, blade-like leaves. Wiry, tan stems emerge through the foliage tipped with tan seedheads.

Features: brilliant blue foliage; decorative, spiked seedheads **Flower color:** tan **Height:** 24–36" **Spread:** 24–30" **Hardiness:** zones 3–8

Bugleweed

Ajuga

Often labeled as a rampant runner, bugleweed grows best where it can roam freely without competition.

Growing

Bugleweed develops the best leaf color in **partial or light shade** but tolerates full shade. The leaves may become scorched when exposed to too much sun. Any **well-drained** soil is suitable. Divide this vigorous plant any time during the growing season.

Remove any new growth or seedlings that don't show the hybrid leaf coloring.

Tips

Bugleweed makes an excellent groundcover for difficult sites, such as exposed slopes and dense shade. It also looks attractive in shrub borders, where its dense growth prevents the spread of all but the most tenacious weeds.

A. reptans 'Pat's Selection' (above)
A. reptans 'Caitlin's Giant' (below)

Recommended

A. genevensis (Geneva bugleweed) is an upright, non-invasive species that bears blue, white or pink spring flowers.

A. pyramidalis 'Metallica Crispa' (upright bugleweed) is a very slow-growing plant with metallic, bronzy brown, crinkly foliage and violet blue flowers.

A. reptans (common bugleweed) is a low, quick-spreading groundcover. Its many cultivars are often chosen over the species for their colorful, often variegated foliage.

Bugleweed combines well with hostas and ferns; it enjoys the same shady sites and growing conditions.

Features: late-spring to early-summer flowers; colorful foliage
Flower color: purple, blue, pink, white; grown for decorative foliage **Height:** 3–12" **Spread:** 6–36" **Hardiness:** zones 3–8

English Ivy
Hedera

H. helix (above & below)

One of the loveliest things about English ivy is the variation in green and blue tones it adds to the garden.

English ivy is also a popular houseplant and is frequently used in topiaries.

Growing

English ivy prefers **light shade** or **partial shade** but will adapt to any light conditions, from full shade to full sun. The foliage can become damaged or dried out in winter if the plant is grown in a sunny, exposed site. The soil should be of **average to rich fertility, moist** and **well drained**. The richer the soil, the better English ivy will grow.

Tips

English ivy is grown as a trailing groundcover or as a climbing vine. It clings tenaciously to house walls, tree trunks, stumps and many other rough-textured surfaces. Ivy rootlets can damage walls and fences, but cold winters prevent the rampant growth that makes this plant troublesome and invasive in warmer climates.

Recommended

H. helix is a vigorous plant with dark, glossy, triangular, evergreen leaves that may be tinged with bronze or purple in winter, adding another season of interest to your garden. Many cultivars have been developed, some for increased cold hardiness. Other cultivars have interesting, often variegated foliage, but are not exceptionally hardy. 'Thorndale' ('Sub-Zero') has dark green, heart-shaped leaves with pale green to white upper veins but only in winter. Check with your local garden center to see what is available.

Also called: common ivy **Features:** foliage; climbing or trailing habit **Height:** indefinite **Spread:** indefinite **Hardiness:** zones 5–8

Eulalia Grass

Miscanthus

Eulalia grass is one of the most popular and majestic of all the ornamental grasses. Its graceful foliage dances in the wind and makes an impressive sight all year round.

Growing

Eulalia grass prefers **full sun**. The soil should be of **average fertility**, **moist** and **well drained**, though some selections also tolerate wet soil. All selections are drought tolerant once established.

Tips

Give these magnificent beauties room to spread so you can fully appreciate their form. The plant's height will determine the best place for each selection in a border. They create dramatic impact in groups or as seasonal screens.

Recommended

There are many available cultivars of *M. sinensis*, all distinguished by the white midrib on the leaf blade. Some popular selections include '**Gracillimus**' (maiden grass), with long, fine-textured leaves; '**Grosse Fontaine**' (large fountain), a tall, wide-spreading, early-flowering selection; '**Morning Light**' (variegated maiden grass), a short and delicate plant with fine, white leaf edges; '**Purpureus**' (flame grass), with foliage that turns bright orange in early fall; '**Silberfeder**' (silver feather), a tall cultivar with silvery white plumes; '**Strictus**' (porcupine grass), a tall, stiff, upright selection with unusual horizontal yellow bands; and

'Purpureus' (above), 'Zebrinus' (below)

'**Zebrinus**' (zebra grass), which has golden yellow, banded, green leaves and coppery pink plumes when young.

Eulalia grass is a warm-season grass, which allows it to tolerate extreme heat and humidity levels.

Also called: Japanese silver grass
Features: upright, arching habit; colorful summer and fall foliage; late-summer and fall flowers; winter interest **Flower color:** pink, copper, silver **Height:** 4–8' **Spread:** 2–4'
Hardiness: zones 5–8, possibly zone 4

Flowering Fern

Osmunda

O. regalis (above & below)

Ferns have a certain prehistoric mystique and can add a graceful elegance and textural accent to the garden.

Growing

Flowering ferns prefer **light shade** but tolerate full sun if the soil is consistently moist. The soil should be **fertile, humus rich, acidic** and **moist**. Flowering ferns tolerate wet soil and will spread as offsets form at the plant bases.

Tips

These large ferns form an attractive mass when planted in large colonies. They can be included in beds and borders and make a welcome addition to a woodland garden.

Recommended

O. cinnamomea (cinnamon fern) has light green fronds that fan out in a circular fashion from a central point. Bright green, leafless, fertile fronds that mature to cinnamon brown are produced in spring and stand straight up in the center of the plant.

O. regalis (royal fern) forms a dense clump of foliage. Feathery, flower-like, fertile fronds stand out among the sterile fronds in summer and mature to a rusty brown. '**Purpurescens**' fronds are purple red when they emerge in spring and then mature to green. This contrasts well with the purple stems. (Zones 3–8)

The flowering fern's 'flowers' are actually its spore-producing sporangia.

Features: perennial deciduous fern; decorative, fertile fronds; habit **Height:** 30"–5'
Spread: 24–36" **Hardiness:** zones 2–8

Japanese Painted Fern

Athyrium

A. *nipponicum* 'Pictum' (above & below)

Japanese painted ferns are striking plants that add wonderful color to an otherwise shady, green landscape.

Growing

Japanese painted fern requires **partial shade** in order to maintain its colorful foliage. If it is planted in full shade, the color may not develop, whereas full sun will cause the color to fade or the leaves to scorch. The soil should be **moderately fertile, moist, neutral to acidic** and **humus rich**. Divide in spring when necessary.

It is important to apply a thick layer of mulch in fall to maintain a better moisture level around the roots and to protect the crown from exposure.

Tips

Japanese painted fern looks very attractive planted en masse in mixed borders or shade gardens. The interesting foliage stands out among other ferns in a woodland setting.

Recommended

A. felix-femina (lady fern) produces lacy-looking, bright green fronds which form a dense mound of foliage. Cultivars offer different forms, sizes and degrees of ornamentation.

A. nipponicum is a creeping, compact fern that bears long, mid-green fronds with reddish purple midribs. The cultivars are far more readily available and attractive than the species. They come in a variety of foliage colors, with new additions appearing yearly.

Plants grown from spores show more varied foliage coloration than those grown from divisions.

Features: attractive foliage **Flower color:** grown for foliage
Height: 6–24" **Spread:** 8–24" **Hardiness:** zones 4–8

Japanese Spurge
Pachysandra

P. terminalis (above & below)

Low-maintenance Japanese spurge is one of the most popular groundcovers around. Its rhizomatous rootzone colonizes quickly to form a dense blanket over the ground.

Growing

Japanese spurge prefers **light to full shade** but tolerates partial shade. Any soil that is **moist, acidic, humus rich** and **well drained** is good. Plants can be propagated easily from cuttings or by division.

Tips

Japanese spurge is a durable groundcover under trees, in shady borders and in woodland gardens. The foliage is considered evergreen but winter-scorched shoots may need to be removed in spring. Shear or mow old plantings in early spring to rejuvenate them.

Recommended

P. terminalis (Japanese spurge) forms a low mass of foliage rosettes. It grows about 8" tall and can spread almost indefinitely. There are a few cultivars to choose from, including **'Green Carpet,'** which is a compact cultivar with smaller, toothed leaves. A variegated cultivar is also available.

Interplant this popular groundcover with spring bulbs, hostas or ferns, or use it as an underplanting for deciduous trees and shrubs with contrasting foliage colors.

Features: perennial, evergreen groundcover; habit; inconspicuous, fragrant spring flowers
Flower color: white **Height:** 6–8" **Spread:** 24" or more **Hardiness:** zones 3–8

Maidenhair Fern

Adiantum

A. pedatum (above & below)

This charming, delicate-looking fern adds grace to any woodland planting. For a touch of whimsy, tuck a garden gnome or other small ornament beneath the fronds to peer out at passers-by.

Growing

Maidenhair fern grows well in **light or partial shade** but tolerates full shade. The soil should be of **average fertility**, **humus rich** and **moist**. It rarely needs dividing but can be divided in spring to propagate more plants.

There are many more species of maidenhair fern but most are grown in greenhouses or as houseplants because they are not hardy to cooler conditions.

Tips

This lovely fern graces any shaded spot in the garden. Include it in rock or woodland gardens and shaded borders, or beneath shade trees where the grass grows thin if it grows at all. It also looks attractive next to a shaded water feature.

Recommended

A. pedatum forms a spreading mound of delicate, arching fronds. Light green leaflets stand out against the black stems, and the whole plant turns bright yellow in fall.

Also called: northern maidenhair
Features: perennial fern; summer and fall foliage; habit **Height:** 12–24"
Spread: 12–24" **Hardiness:** zones 2–8

Myrtle
Vinca

V. minor (above & below)

Commonly known as an evergreen groundcover plant, myrtle is far more than that. Its reliability is second to none, and its ease of growth is sure to please.

Growing

Grow myrtle in **partial to full shade**. It will grow in **any type** of soil, but it will turn yellow if the soil is too dry or the sun is too hot. Divide myrtle in early spring or mid- to late fall, or whenever it is becoming overgrown. One plant can cover almost any size of area.

Tips

Myrtle is a useful and attractive groundcover in a shrub border, under trees or on a shady bank, and it prevents soil erosion. It is shallow-rooted and able to out-compete weeds but won't interfere with deeper-rooted shrubs.

If myrtle begins to outgrow its space, it may be sheared back hard in early spring. The sheared-off ends may have rooted along the stems. These rooted cuttings may be potted and given away as gifts, or may be introduced to new areas of the garden.

Recommended

V. minor (lesser periwinkle) forms a low, loose mat of trailing stems. Purple or blue flowers are borne in a flush in spring and sporadically throughout summer. '**Alba**' bears white flowers; '**Atropurpurea**' bears reddish purple flowers; and '**Bowles Series**' of cultivars offer flowers in shades of white and blue.

Features: trailing foliage; mid-spring to fall flowers
Flower color: purple, blue, white, reddish purple
Height: 4–8" **Spread:** indefinite **Hardiness:** zones 4–8

Ostrich Fern

Matteuccia

M. struthiopteris (above & below)

Ostrich ferns are prized for their delicious, emerging spring fronds as well as for their ornamental foliage and habit.

Growing

Ostrich fern prefers **partial or light shade** but tolerates full shade. The soil should be **average to fertile, humus rich, neutral to acidic** and **moist**.

The tightly coiled new spring fronds taste delicious lightly steamed and served with butter. Remove the bitter, papery, reddish brown coating before steaming.

Also called: fiddlehead fern
Features: perennial fern; foliage; habit
Height: 3–5' **Spread:** 12–36" or more
Hardiness: zones 1–8

Tips

This fern appreciates a moist woodland garden and is often found growing wild along the edges of woodland streams and creeks. Useful in shaded borders, this plant is quick to spread—a delight to those who have tasted the delicate, young fronds.

Recommended

M. struthiopteris (*M. pennsylvanica*) forms a circular cluster of slightly arching fronds. Stiff, brown, fertile fronds poke up in the center of the cluster in late summer and persist through winter.

Reed Grass

Calamagrostis

'Overdam' (above), 'Karl Foerster' (below)

Reed grass is highly sought after and is frequently used by landscape designers who appreciate its upright, architectural appearance.

This is a graceful, metamorphic grass that changes its habit and flower color throughout the seasons. The slightest breeze keeps this grass in perpetual motion.

Growing

Reed grass thrives in **full to partial sun**. The soil should be **moist**, **humus rich** and **well drained**. It is tolerant of even the poorest soils.

Tips

Reed grass is ideal for mixed borders and xeriscaped spaces. The long, elegant inflorescences last well into the following spring and add beauty to a winter landscape.

Cut all stems down to the crown or to the ground in early spring. This will allow for new growth as the days become warmer.

Recommended

C. x *acutiflora* is a slow-growing perennial that grows into a clump of arching, narrow, green blades of grass. Tall, wiry stems emerge through the clump, bearing silvery bronze to pale purple-brown panicles of flowers. Decorative cultivars are available in varied sizes and colors, including **'Karl Foerster,'** a Perennial Plant of the Year winner for 2001, bearing tall, decorative seedheads.

Also called: smallweed, feather reed grass **Features:** decorative flower stems; foliage; habit **Height:** 2–5' **Spread:** 2–4' **Hardiness:** zones 3–8

Spotted Dead Nettle

Lamium

L. maculatum 'Anne Greenaway' (above), *L. maculatum* 'Beacon Silver' (below)

This attractive plant, with its striped, dotted or banded silver and green foliage, hugs the ground and thrives on only the barest necessities of life.

Growing

Spotted dead nettle prefers **partial to light shade**. It tolerates full sun but may become leggy. The soil should be of **average fertility, humus rich, moist** and **well drained**. The more fertile the soil, the more vigorously the plant will grow. It is drought tolerant in shade but develops bare patches if the soil dries out for extended periods. Divide and replant in fall if bare spots become unsightly.

Spotted dead nettle remains more compact if sheared back after flowering. If it remains green over winter, shear back in early spring.

Tips

Spotted dead nettle plants make useful groundcovers for woodland or shade gardens. They also help keep weeds down under shrubs in a border.

Recommended

L. galeobdolon (*Lamiastrum galeobdolon;* yellow archangel) can be invasive, though the cultivars are less so. The yellow flowers bloom in spring to early summer. Several cultivars are available.

L. maculatum (spotted dead nettle) is the most commonly grown dead nettle. This low-growing, spreading species has green leaves with white or silvery markings and bears white, pink or mauve flowers. Many cultivars are available.

Also called: dead nettle, lamium **Features:** spring or summer flowers; decorative, often variegated foliage
Flower color: white, pink, yellow, mauve; plant also grown for foliage **Height:** 6–24" **Spread:** 12–24" **Hardiness:** zones 2–8

Sweet Woodruff

Galium

G. odoratum (above & below)

Sweet woodruff is a groundcover that abounds with good qualities, including attractive, light green foliage that smells like new-mown hay, abundant, white, spring flowers and the ability to fill in garden spaces without taking over.

The dried leaves of sweet woodruff were once used to scent bed linens and freshen stale rooms.

Growing

This plant prefers **partial shade**. It will grow well, but will not bloom well, in full shade. The soil should be **humus rich** and evenly **moist**.

Tips

Sweet woodruff is a perfect woodland groundcover. It forms a beautiful, green carpet and thrives in the same conditions as azaleas and rhododendrons. Shear it back after it blooms to encourage growth of foliage that will crowd out weeds.

Recommended

G. odoratum is a low, spreading groundcover. Clusters of star-shaped, white flowers are borne in a flush in late spring and appear sporadically through mid-summer.

Features: perennial groundcover; late-spring to mid-summer flowers; fragrant foliage; habit **Flower color:** white **Height:** 12–18"
Spread: indefinite **Hardiness:** zones 3–8

Switch Grass

Panicum

*A*native to the prairie grasslands, switch grass naturalizes equally well in an informal border or a natural meadow.

Growing

Switch grass thrives in **full sun, light shade** or **partial shade.** The soil should be of **average fertility** and **well drained**, though plants adapt to both moist and dry soils and tolerate conditions ranging from heavy clay to lighter sandy soil. Cut switch grass back to 2–4" from the ground in early spring. The flower stems may break under heavy, wet snow or in exposed, windy sites.

Tips

Plant switch grass singly in small gardens, in large groups in spacious borders or at the edges of ponds or pools for a dramatic, whimsical effect. The seedheads attract birds and the foliage changes color in fall, so place this plant where you can enjoy both features.

'Warrior' (above), 'Heavy Metal' (below)

The delicate, airy panicles of switch grass fill in the gaps in a garden border, and they can be cut for fresh or dried arrangements.

Recommended

P. virgatum (switch grass) is suited to wild meadow gardens. Some of its popular cultivars include **'Heavy Metal'** (blue switch grass), an upright plant with narrow, steely blue foliage flushed with gold and burgundy in fall; **'Northwind,'** a narrow, tall grass with olive-green foliage and beautiful, golden fall color; **'Prairie Sky'** (blue switch grass), an arching plant with deep blue foliage; and **'Shenandoah'** (red switch grass), which has red-tinged, green foliage that turns burgundy in fall.

Features: clumping habit; green, blue or burgundy foliage; airy panicles of flowers; fall color; winter interest
Height: 3–5' **Spread:** 30–36" **Hardiness:** zones 3–8

Wild Ginger

Asarum

A. canadense (above), *A. europaeum* (below)

Wild ginger is a beautiful ground-cover for woodland sites. Glossy, heart-shaped leaves form a low-growing mat that grows quickly but is not invasive.

Growing

Wild ginger needs **full or partial shade**. The soil should be **moist** and **humus rich**. All *Asarum* species prefer **acidic** soils, but *A. canadense* will tolerate alkaline conditions. Wild ginger tolerates dry conditions for a while in good shade, but prolonged drought will eventually cause wilt and dieback.

Tips

Plant wild ginger in a shady rock garden, border or woodland garden. Wild ginger is relatively easy to remove from places where it isn't welcome.

Recommended

A. canadense (Canada wild ginger) has slightly hairy, heart-shaped leaves. The roots of this wild ginger can be used in place of true ginger (*Zingiber officinale*) in recipes.

A. europaeum (European wild ginger) forms an expanding clump of very glossy leaves, often distinctively silver-veined. This species is not as heat tolerant as *A. canadense*.

Wild ginger flowers have a unique shape, an unusual brown-maroon color and an unpleasant, slightly fetid odor that attracts their beetle pollinators.

Features: attractive foliage; easy to grow
Height: 3–6" **Spread:** 12" or more
Hardiness: zones 4–8

Wintercreeper

Euonymus

The versatile and adaptable wintercreeper, with species ranging from deciduous shrubs to evergreen climbers, can fill a number of roles in the landscape.

Growing

Wintercreeper prefers **full sun** but tolerates light or partial shade. Soil of **average to rich fertility** is preferable but any **moist, well-drained** soil will do.

Tips

Wintercreeper can be grown as a hedge or as a shrub in a border. It makes an excellent substitute for the more demanding boxwood. Its trailing habit also makes it useful as a groundcover or climber.

Recommended

E. fortunei (wintercreeper euonymus) as a species is rarely grown; its wide and attractive variety of cultivars are much more popular. These can be prostrate, climbing or mounding evergreens, often with handsome, variegated foliage, including 'Coloratus' (purple-leaf wintercreeper), which produces dark green foliage that changes to a reddish purple in fall.

'Emerald 'n' Gold' (above)

Features: foliage; fall color; habit **Habit:** groundcover; low growing **Height:** 18–24" **Spread:** indefinite **Hardiness:** zones 3–8

Wood Fern

Dryopteris

D. marginalis (above)

Reliable, hardy, tough and eye-catching ferns are all included in this grouping of wood ferns.

Growing

Wood ferns thrive in **partial shade** in a sheltered location. The soil should be **moist** and **humus rich.**

The genus Dryopteris *is made up of 225 species of moisture-loving, shady woodland ferns native to temperate regions around the world.*

Tips

On average, wood ferns are of medium size and are most effective when planted in small groups or en masse in shade gardens or woodland settings. They're also a beautiful complement to other shade-loving plants, including hostas, coral bells and cranesbill.

Recommended

D. filix-mas (male fern) is a deciduous fern that produces tall, arching, triangular, finely cut, bright green fronds. This native fern is more tolerant of sun where soil is evenly moist at all times. Its overall appearance is delicate and lacy, almost soft to the touch. Cultivars offer slender, upright versions of the species or compact forms with delicately detailed fronds that contrast beautifully with bolder-leaved perennials.

D. marginalis (leather wood fern, marginal wood fern) is native to most of northeastern North America. It produces a clump of leathery, green fronds that may remain evergreen in some regions, but it benefits from a trim in late winter.

Also called: buckler fern, shield fern **Features:** decorative fronds; habit; form; use **Height:** 1–4' **Spread:** 12–36" **Hardiness:** zones 2–8

Glossary

Acid soil: soil with a pH lower than 7.0

Annual: a plant that germinates, flowers, sets seed and dies in one growing season

Alkaline soil: soil with a pH higher than 7.0

Basal leaves: leaves that form from the crown, at the base of the plant

Bract: a modified leaf at the base of a flower or flower cluster

Corm: a bulb-like, food-storing, underground stem, resembling a bulb without scales

Crown: the part of the plant at or just below soil level where the shoots join the roots

Cultivar: a cultivated plant variety with one or more distinct differences from the species, e.g., in flower color or disease resistance

Damping off: fungal disease causing seedlings to rot at soil level and topple over

Deadhead: to remove spent flowers to maintain a neat appearance and encourage a longer blooming season

Direct sow: to sow seeds directly in the garden

Dormancy: a period of plant inactivity, usually during winter or unfavorable conditions

Double flower: a flower with an unusually large number of petals

Genus: a category of biological classification between the species and family levels; the first word in a scientific name indicates the genus

Grafting: a type of propagation in which a stem or bud of one plant is joined onto the rootstock of another plant of a closely related species

Hardy: capable of surviving unfavorable conditions, such as cold weather or frost, without protection

Hip: the fruit of a rose, containing the seeds

Humus: decomposed or decomposing organic material in the soil

Hybrid: a plant resulting from natural or human-induced cross-breeding between varieties, species or genera

Inflorescence: a flower cluster

Male clone: a plant that may or may not produce pollen but that will not produce fruit, seed or seedpods

Neutral soil: soil with a pH of 7.0

Perennial: a plant that takes three or more years to complete its life cycle

pH: a measure of acidity or alkalinity; the soil pH influences availability of nutrients for plants

Rhizome: a root-like, food-storing stem that grows horizontally at or just below soil level, from which new shoots may emerge

Rootball: the root mass and surrounding soil of a plant

Seedhead: dried, inedible fruit that contains seeds; the fruiting stage of the inflorescence

Self-seeding: reproducing by means of seeds without human assistance, so that new plants constantly replace those that die

Semi-double flower: a flower with petals in two or three rings

Single flower: a flower with a single ring of typically four or five petals

Species: the fundamental unit of biological classification; the entity from which cultivars and varieties are derived

Standard: a shrub or small tree grown with an erect main stem, accomplished either through pruning and training or by grafting the plant onto a tall, straight stock

Sucker: a shoot that comes up from the root, often some distance from the plant; it can be separated to form a new plant once it develops its own roots

Tender: incapable of surviving the climatic conditions of a given region and requiring protection from frost or cold

Tuber: the thick section of a rhizome bearing nodes and buds

Variegation: foliage that has more than one color, often patched or striped or bearing leaf margins of a different color

Variety: a naturally occurring variant of a species

Index of Plant Names

Entries in **bold** type indicate the main plant headings.

Author Biographies

Chuck Porto's horticultural roots began as a child in West Des Moines, Iowa, helping his family cultivate a 1.5 acre garden and sell vegetables out of their garage and to various restaurants. He is a graduate of Dowling High School in West Des Moines, and the University of Iowa. Chuck has been in the garden center and nursery business for 17 years, and he is an Iowa Certified Nursery Professional. In January 2003, he became the host of KXIC's *Saturday Lawn & Garden Show*, a local informational and call-in show. In 2004, Chuck became an adjunct instructor at Kirkwood Community College in Cedar Rapids, Iowa, teaching Integrated Pest Management. Chuck lives, works and gardens in Iowa City.

Laura Peters is a certified Master Gardener with 15 gardening books to her credit. She has gained valuable experience in every aspect of the horticultural industry in a career that has spanned more than 16 years. She enjoys sharing her practical knowledge of organic gardening, plant varieties and gardening products with fellow gardeners.

Acknowledgments

I would like to thank Laura Peters and Lone Pine Publishing for giving me the opportunity to be involved in this book; it has been a truly enjoyable experience. I would also like to thank my parents, Charlie and Lucille, for putting me here and giving me guidance. Special thanks to my daughter Amanda and to my wife Mary, my partner in life and gardening. — *Chuck Porto*

A big thanks to my family and friends for their endless encouragement and support all these years. I would also like to thank Chuck Porto. Without his expertise and assistance, this book would have lacked that Iowa touch. A special thanks also goes to those who allowed me to photograph their lovely gardens and to those who kindly offered their beautiful images, including Michelle Meyer from Bailey Nurseries, Brendan Casement, Conard-Pyle Roses and David Austin Roses. — *Laura Peters*